KT-412-920

TEACH YOURSELF BOOKS

CYBERNETICS

This book is intended to outline for the beginner the ramifications of the science of 'Cybernetics'. It is a science concerned with all matters of control and communication and to this extent trespasses across what we have come to think of as the established sciences. The book covers both the pure theory of Cybernetics—mathematical, statistical and logical, and its application, which affects everything human beings do, especially how they learn, how they make decisions, how they plan, and how they solve problems, in such fields as Engineering, Management and Education.

TEACH YOURSELF BOOKS

CYBERNETICS

F. H. GEORGE

TEACH YOURSELF BOOKS

ST. PAUL'S HOUSE WARWICK LANE LONDON EC4

First printed   1971

Filmset by Keyspools Ltd, Golborne, Lancs.
Printed by C. Tinling & Co. Ltd, Prescot and London

ISBN 0 340 05941 9

CONTENTS

CHAPTER ONE

BASIC IDEAS IN CYBERNETICS

ARGUMENT

Cybernetics is a science with a difference. Unlike subjects such as Botany, Zoology or Physics, it has no long-standing and well-defined domain of activity. It is concerned with all matters of control and communication, and to this extent trespasses across what we have come to think of as the established sciences.

Cybernetics has, however, a reasonably well-defined *pure* and *applied* side to its activities. The pure theory is mainly abstract—mathematical, statistical and logical—whereas the applied side is relevant to everything human beings do, especially how they learn, how they make decisions, how they plan and how they solve problems. Cybernetics also applies to the contexts in which they perform, as in Engineering Cybernetics, Management Cybernetics and Educational Cybernetics.

This book is intended to outline, for the beginner, the ramifications of the science of 'Cybernetics'.

There is always a great deal of discussion as to what the word 'Cybernetics' means. No one answer satisfies everyone, partly because any subject can be described at various levels of complexity. The classic example of this question of degree of detail is that of 'electricity'; this means, for the householder, knowing how to switch on lights: for the electrician, knowing how to mend fuses and repair wiring defects, but for the physicist it is part of an abstract theory of matter. What explanation we give depends on the context and the use to which the answer has to be put.

One can also place emphasis on the research side of the subject or on its applications; in the case of cybernetics the first may seem abstract but the second is certainly concrete. Just to make matters more complicated there are various ways of defining terms apart from the degree of complexity which they carry; so if a definition is required then the problem is that much more difficult. We will start therefore with some abstract statements and then become more concrete, and leave the reader to select the level of approach he finds most helpful. The reader should always remember that we are trying, for the sake of clarity, to talk in the simplest terms.

Cybernetics is the science of control and communication, with special reference to *self-controlling* or *adaptive* systems. It does not draw an absolute distinction between organisms and inanimate, or man-made, systems in this context, since either *can* be self-controlling and adaptive in behaviour.

In the case of a man it is fairly obvious that he is adaptive and capable of learning, since he is always learning to do things in new, and often better, ways. But in recent years we have discovered that we can also make machines (appropriately programmed computers are the best known example) which change their behaviour as a result of a change in their environment. *George*, the automatic pilot, is one well known machine based on such an adaptive principle.

Since cybernetics is a science, it attempts to provide a precise theory of adaptive systems of all sizes and kinds, and of different degrees of complexity.

In practice, cybernetics cuts across the so-called established sciences such as physics, chemistry, zoology, etc. by abstracting those common features which contribute to an integrated theory of control and communication.

The adaptive feature suggests *negative feedback* as a vital factor, and while this reminds us of servo-systems at one level, it reminds us of human learning in the light of 'knowledge of results' at another level. Negative feedback channels output back to modify input, much as a car driver steers his car by watching his position relative to the road, making corrective movements by use of his steering wheel, *George*, the automatic pilot to which we referred, is basically a servo-system. Servo-systems have an output signal which controls some process, and a sensing device which records a change in the environment, say a change of temperature or pressure, and this change *automatically* changes the output signal. There is a whole class of such systems, of greatly varying complexity. We shall discuss some of them in this book.

The theoretical properties of the more mathematical features of cybernetics are embodied in fields known as *automata theory*, *recursive function theory*, *Turing machines* (part of automata theory) and *metamathematics* generally. This last includes the study of automata and recursive function theory, which is concerned with supplying a clearcut foundation for mathematics in axiomatic form. Discussions of the foundations of mathematics are relevant to our problem, as we shall see.

Their relevancy lies in the limitations which we now know apply to axiomatic systems. Axiomatic systems are precise systems based on assumptions. They are usually in mathematical form or stated in ordinary language. Euclid's geometry is probably still the best known axiomatic system. We shall explain later the significance for cybernetics of such axiomatic systems.

We could sensibly divide cybernetics into its pure and applied aspects, although the division is fairly arbitrary. On the applied side, we would think of servomechanisms and control machinery as within engineering cybernetics. The mathematical techniques mentioned in the last paragraph, and to be explained later, makes up a part of mathematical cybernetics. Similarly in Chapter XI we discuss teaching machines and other aspects of educational cybernetics. Experiments in social, behavioural and decision-taking-and-planning activities define social, behavioural and management cybernetics respectively.

There are other approaches to these problems. Bionics is the study of engineering systems which imitate organisms. Biocybernetics and bionics are almost the same subject.

The pure side of cybernetics is concerned with feedback systems and their properties and is closely allied to general systems theory, which is a discipline with a separate history, and which, like pure cybernetics, tends to talk in terms of systems and their properties.

One of the central problems of cybernetics is artificial intelligence. Can machines be made to show intelligence and if so, to what extent? The reason axiomatic systems are relevant is because they are, in effect, theoretical machines. Much of our mathematical theory tells us what some kind of machine would do without actually building it. It is enough that we have the blueprint for the machine, and we can understand the behaviour from the blueprint alone. This is fortunate because the machines in which we are interested are very large and very expensive to produce.

The word 'machine' provides in these discussions a special difficulty, particularly when featured in such issues as 'could machines be made to think?' We clearly do not mean 'machine' here to apply merely to those machine-like systems such as motor cars or aeroplanes, which by very definition of the word 'machine-like' are non-thinking. We now mean 'machine' to include anything capable of being 'made in the laboratory' and made by man—at least 'made by man' in the first instance.

Some people think of cybernetics as the artificial construction of human beings, whether by artificial seeds that then grow into an embryo and then a human being, or directly. To do either is at present outside our capabilities, but arguments still persist about the possibility of doing so 'in principle'. Such discussions are important because the most useful part of pursuing such apparently grandiose goals is not necessarily the final achievement, which *may never* occur, but the 'fall out' which occurs en route.

Such human-like systems draw attention to the properties of adaptive systems in general, which help us to understand how a business ticks, and how governments operate, and other such particular, but vital, problems. A commercial firm or a government, or indeed any social group, is sufficiently like an organism for many of the same principles to apply to both; this is what cybernetics is especially concerned with, in this context.

At the more abstract level of cybernetics, and as a result of investigating the 'bits and pieces' of our total cybernetic program, we now know a great deal more about how people think, take decisions, perform logic, use language and show intelligence in all sorts of ways. Here cybernetics overlaps psychology, philosophy and logic, as well as semantics and mathematics.

As a result of these studies, we can set up models, especially in the form of computer programs which can perform some parts of the intelligent behaviour described. These parts are gradually being combined so that the same program, or set of interrelated programs, can accept data, whether in linguistic form or otherwise; it can also formulate concepts and hypotheses and test them. This clearly is the beginning of a model of human intelligence and, although it lacks human flexibility, provided it is geared into a sufficiently narrow sector of knowledge it has great advantages over the human being.

The advantages it possesses are above all those of speed and accuracy, and this reflects once more the extraordinary versatility of the digital computer. The main reasons the digital computer comes into the picture are:

1. Theories about what can be done on a computer are also relevant to other systems capable of being made (or of growing) to the point of showing degrees of intelligence.

2. The computer is one of the few sufficiently large universal machines. If ingeniously programmed it can be made to copy (simulate) almost anything, including human, or human-like, intelligence.

It should be made clear that the theory of cybernetics in no way depends upon digital computers. The hardware construction of cybernetic models can take the form of structures like nerve cells which are made electronically, or of chemicals; they can be analogue computers; or they can be any 'special purpose' equipment which mirrors in some way communication and control properties of adaptive systems whether human-like or completely unhuman-like. Also included in cybernetics is the study of 'natural' control and communication systems such as are involved, for example, in the musculature of organisms, the physiology of the internal organs and, in particular, of the nervous system. The study of genetics is relevant to cybernetic 'growth' models, and there are various theories of machine reproduction which (as one might reasonably expect) bear a close relationship to some genetic theories.

Cybernetics operates also at the applied level, and here the technique of *heuristic programming* is most relevant to cybernetics. By a 'heuristic', we mean here an approximation, shortcut, or a rough-and-ready method. Perhaps in general the best synonym for 'heuristic' is 'hypothesis'. Heuristic programming is the use of computer programs which incorporate such heuristics. These heuristics can be thought of as models, or like maps of territory, but are always in some way made approximate.

We all know that payroll, ledger keeping, accounts, the use of statistical and mathematical methods and a whole host of similar procedures can be carried out on the computer. What is less known is that 'off the cuff' decisions and plans can also be programmed on to a computer.

The process of *ad hoc* programming, which we call heuristic, is of the utmost importance. If we were asked to hit upon the solution to a combination lock, we know, because the number of possible combinations are finite, that we *can* find the solution, but it may take months, or even years. If we were asked to forecast exactly how many articles of a certain kind we would sell next month, then we could not give a precise solution, except by guessing and hoping the guess is a good one. Both these cases call for heuristic methods, since in the first case it is not economic to use the 'precise' method of exhaustive search, and in the second case no 'precise' method is possible.

The computer uses heuristics, which, as we have said, are short cuts, hypotheses or models. They are adaptive so that when mistakes are made, they are remedied (hopefully) for the next time, and the whole process is fast, *explicit*, making the best possible use of all the available information.

Such heuristic methods apply to a military commander taking decisions in a war, or to a Board of Directors deciding whether to expand one section of the business, or to close another section; to build a new factory or to shut up a particular part of an old factory. Mathematical heuristics for modelling demand and providing estimates of sales are already well known. The non-mathematical types of heuristics are much less well known.

It is possible, as a result of the development of heuristics, for the management of a company to make their decisions quickly and efficiently, at the same time steadily improving their standards. This is once more the subject we have called Management Cybernetics.

We can program a computer to converse in ordinary English or something close to it, using typewriters rather than voices; this provides for quick and efficient data retrieval and inference making. This facility dovetails perfectly with the heuristic one and with the process of explicitly learning by experience. When experience is not possible—where 'one off' decisions are called for—then *simulation* techniques are available. These techniques involve building a model of the system and testing the model instead of testing the system.

If you have a system, whether a mechanical toy, an industry, a string of retail shops, a defence radar network or a human being, provided it is adaptive and capable of accumulating knowledge in simple or complex ways, then its study is central to cybernetics.

SUMMARY
One of the central problems of cybernetics is artificial
intelligence. Artificial intelligence depends upon concept
and hypothesis formation, logic, heuristics, and the use
of ordinary language and of models which mirror all
these activities collectively.

We shall expect to find many different modelling
methods, but the most important vehicle for modelling
is the digital computer. This is because of its size, speed
and accuracy, and its economy of method.

CHAPTER TWO
SELF-ADAPTING SYSTEMS

ARGUMENT

Self-adapting systems are systems which are self-modifying in the sense we have already discussed, in Chapter 1, in the case of *George*; they change as a function of their changing environment, and they can be described and constructed in many different ways.

Some self-adapting systems have been described in mathematical, statistical or logical terms; this has been so with a view to *simulating* (or copying) organisms. Others have been constructed in a purely abstract way, where the aim has been to *synthesize* (achieve the same end product by whatever means) some, usually 'intelligent', system.

Self-adapting systems have important properties of stability ('ultra-stability' is the word sometimes used) which mark them off as being different from inanimate or non-adaptive systems. It allows them to become goal-seeking, or purposive, seeking the goal of stability.

Servo-systems, automatic control systems and computers are all examples of self-adapting systems, and these self-adapting systems can be described either in terms of precise information or in terms of probabilities. Whichever is used, the ultimate aim is always to supply models, in some form, of intelligent processes.

Self-adapting systems

Cybernetics is inter-disciplinary, in that, as we have already indicated, it derives its background from a variety of different sciences, as well as mathematics, logic and philosophy. In fact, the historical background of cybernetics lies explicitly in mathematics, physiology, electrical engineering, especially computer engineering, psychology and sociology. Indeed the whole of theoretical biology is to some extent bound up with the biological aspects of cybernetic thinking.

It is the inter-disciplinary nature of cybernetics which has created many difficulties for its development. Anything that is, by its nature, very general, cutting across the accepted boundaries of any 'chunk of knowledge', especially science, is likely to leave its practitioners open to criticism. This is so because they are dealing in terms of the established sciences and will often deal with them in a more superficial, and certainly different, way from the specialist scientists themselves. This is a problem the cybernetician faces in the same way as the philosopher of science or the scientific theorist.

We have already mentioned servo-systems and this is one starting point for cybernetics. The correcting information fed back from the sensing device is called *negative feedback*, and we can think of this, as we mentioned earlier, in the case of the car driver when he makes correcting movements on his steering wheel. We could, of course, talk about cybernetics entirely in terms of negative feed-back, stability or ultra-stability. Think of stability as implying points of equilibrium in a system and it is this equilibrium of a system which supplies the goal of the negative feedback which gives it control.

When thinking of servo-systems, one thinks straight away of something relatively simple like *George* or a Watt governor, which is one of the earliest feed-back devices, in which a signal indicates the speed of the steam engine. This signal is conveyed to a power amplifier device in the form of a steam throttle so that as the engine accelerates the steam applied to it is reduced. As a result of this, of course, the speed of the steam engine is kept steady. It should be mentioned that the signal is independent of the energy and therefore it is a form of information control. In a sense this is the prototype of all cybernetic systems.

It is the negative feed-back of information flow and the storage of information over long periods of time which, in controlling systems, are the basic features of cybernetic interest. **This means that it is the search for, and the endeavour to manufacture, artificial intelligence which is the principal fundamental problem of cybernetics.**

We must emphasize that the whole problem of learning and adaptation, as well as problems of human-like thinking, can be tackled from a great number of stand-points. This means that many different methods could be used and also that many different models can be envisaged, and many of them built.

Pre-wired and Growth Systems

When we talk of servo-systems, we think of them as being adaptive and able to change their state, but we also think of them as being wholly pre-wired; they do not grow. We can, however, study systems like human beings and animals that literally grow in size and complexity.

The distinction between *growth* models and *pre-wired* models has led to much discussion. It has often been argued that if you are simulating organic self-adapting systems, then the model itself must grow and change. On the other hand it has also been argued that if you are simulating adaptive systems you can do this by means of fixed pre-wired systems such as in a computer, or any other system capable of changing its state. The reason for thinking that the pre-wired model (e.g. the computer) is an adequate model for self-adaption, is that on the one hand it is a *universal* model, since it is never complete until its program has been inserted, and on the other that it is the choice of programs which allows for change and self-adaption within the computer. Such programs have sometimes been called 'underspecified' or learning programs, and are clearly adequate for many purposes of cybernetic modelling.

Those who support the growth model view of simulation will sometimes argue that you must have a system, ideally built of chemical and protoplasmic materials; they must somehow be organic to simulate organic systems adequately.

Such organic models actually change their structure as a function of the environment in which they live. The situation is that both types of system or model are acceptable. If one is interested in functional, say physiological, variations and adaptations, then a pre-wired model, capable of showing or including variations, is perfectly adequate. On the other hand if you are interested in anatomical variation then you will ideally use an organic or some sort of physically changing model, although it should be made clear that one can copy 'growth' in a model which is only capable of functional change.

It is important from the point of view of cybernetics to recognise that these views are not inconsistent with each other; they are complementary. What is more important, and what in some measure underlies the discussion about growth and pre-wired models, is the question of how much the maturation (innate structural and anatomical development) and evolution of a model affects its state at any later time. In other words, should we attempt to build ready-made models of some aspect of the adult human being, such as the nervous system, or should we construct a 'seed' which can then be shown to evolve slowly to the adult state? The answer is that we should try to do both.

Whereas the second approach is clearly necessary for anything like a complete biological model, the first is completely adequate to an understanding of the learning of problem-solving or planning, and even clarifies our understanding of a system like the human nervous system. This is especially true where the attempt is primarily to synthesize, rather than to simulate, human behaviour.

Synthesis and Simulation

We have used the words 'synthesis' and 'simulation' frequently, let us now try to clarify further their use.

There are two quite distinct cybernetic problems concerned with synthesis and simulation, and sometimes they have not been sufficiently distinguished. Cyberneticians have been interested in the simulation (copying) of organismic behaviour. They have also been interested in simulating human intelligence. Cyberneticians have also, however, been interested in constructing systems which are capable of learning, thinking, problem-solving and performing the whole range of human-like ability, *without any interest* whatever in simulating human intelligence as such. They are only concerned with the end product when they are synthesizing, and not at all with the means.

This distinction between simulation and synthesis is much the same as the distinction in the field of behaviour between experimental psychology and behavioural cybernetics, although the two fields have a considerable overlap.

It might be argued that any attempt to build an artificially intelligent system must necessarily entail copying human beings' behaviour. This is rather the point of view taken by the scientists who work in bionics, who openly copy organismic behaviour in the design, among other things, of engineering materials. However, it is certainly true to say that we can construct artificial systems which clearly work on quite different materials and principles from those used by human beings. For example, a computer, which can perform most human-like activities, operates on the basis of elements like transistors which are manifestly different from human neurons (nerve cells) in their material construction, although they are functionally very similar in certain ways, or can be made so when organized by a suitable computer program.

At this stage in the development of cybernetics, it is the *functional similarity* of artificial to natural systems which is perhaps the most important factor in cybernetic development. Cyberneticians are generally not concerned about producing their models of the same materials as the original; they are usually more concerned with a method which is functionally similar. In extreme instances, however, the cybernetician does not care whether or not his model has any resemblance to the human being, and judges its effectiveness *only* in terms of the end results; this is what we have called synthesis. It is here, though, we feel that in practice there must be some functional similarity to human intelligence, because in trying to construct a model we are bound in some part to copy the human being and his methods; indeed copying of the methods is usually quite explicit.

The fact remains that we have to distinguish very carefully between cyberneticians who are specifically trying to understand human behaviour or biology by methods of simulation, and cyberneticians who are only interested in synthesizing artificial intelligence systems for planning, or other control purposes, in society; this especially applies to the field of management cybernetics, which we shall discuss later in the book.

The first group, interested in simulation, tend to be

interested in growth models to a far greater extent than the group who are primarily interested in synthesis.

Axiomatic Systems

In cybernetics we are involved in a study of hardware (servos, computers, electronic models, etc.) and software (computer programs, mathematical and statistical models, etc.). We now look again at axiomatic systems which are strictly software, although they can, if necessary, be constructed as hardware.

Axiomatic systems are such that if we start from a set of assumptions, and with a deductive rule of inference, within limits, we can, as with Euclidean's geometry, draw up a series of theorems which we write down one after another. Now it is not obvious that we know in advance all the theorems implied by the assumptions and the rule of inference.

Having built a machine equivalent to an axiomatic system made up of a set of assumptions and a rule of inference, we shall not necessarily know what the machine will do, because we cannot ourselves always see all the implications involved in the action of the rules of inference on the assumptions. By a rule of inference, we mean the ability to draw the conclusion 'I am in Buckinghamshire' from the assumptions 'I am in High Wycombe' and 'High Wycombe is in Buckinghamshire'.

The position is that the principles on which machines can be built, and many of the things they can do, can be studied by axiomatic systems, which, as we have said, are blueprints for machines in hardware.

The need for actually building a machine from the blueprint arises precisely when we are not sure we understand completely the software model; to demonstrate some principle to other people, or to use it to perform some task for us.

Let us next look briefly at the more philosophical issue

of the limitations on machines, approachable through software. We mean, of course, 'machine' in the sense of something that we construct in the laboratory. Such machines are sometimes called *artefacts*.

Limitations on Machines

One limitation that is often cited is that such artefacts could not pursue artistic activities.

It is sufficient at this stage to say that this is not really relevant to the question of learning and the like, which is our primary concern. However, it seems likely that to be able to reproduce anything like the emotions of human beings, machines must be built with the same emotional and motivational systems as those of human beings. The simple answer seems to be that, probably, *the materials used* are vital to the nature of the emotional responses. Until we can build a machine from the same materials as human beings we shall probably never get quite the same sort of emotional responses. In any case, a far greater breadth of experience than is at the moment possible is necessary if machines are to exhibit the same variety of responses. We are assuming here that some form of 'emotional behaviour', which is a sort of alarm, or fuse-box system, is always possible.

These last thoughts lead back to a consideration of the biological side of the matter. Apart from emotions, is there from biological evidence some argument as to why machines cannot think? The interesting point is that there has been, for a very long time, a conflict in biological circles on just this point. The difference of opinion as to whether or not biological explanations should be mechanistic, or depend upon mechanical analogy, is the same argument in another form.

This has been decided, in modern biology, largely in favour of an explanation in terms of machine-like activities. There has been opposition from some biologists and apparent alternatives have been suggested. But these alternatives are generally capable of integration into a mechanistic type of system. At the same time it should be emphasized that the matter is still very much under debate.

As far as psychology is concerned, behaviourism—the school of thought which favours mechanistic arguments—has gained almost complete sway over all other forms of explanation. In psychology, and even in more specifically biological fields, much has been made by way of concession to the original narrow mechanistic views, but now virtually all the explanations used are universally machine-like in character.

We are now led back to the main argument: whether or not machines *could* be capable of thinking. Those scientists and philosophers who have argued that machines are not capable of thinking have, in their argument, overlooked one very important aspect. They usually overlook the fact that human beings have the same sort of drawbacks as machines. If human beings break their parts they may not be in a position to repair themselves, without outside help in the person of a doctor. Furthermore, it is clear that a human being without the necessary nervous system will be as incapable as a machine of carrying out the functions of thinking and imagining; there are many 'medical' instances of this.

We shall make one last point on this difficult matter of whether or not machines could be made to think, and this must suffice. It will only be because of the ingenuity of human beings that 'machines' will be made to think or show intelligent behaviour, and it is because of man's ingenuity that he will be able, in time, to make an artificial system even cleverer than himself. This may not affect the outcome for society or for man. Whoever is responsible, the outcome, whatever that is, will be the same.

We next discuss the main problem categories involved in cybernetic research.

Cybernetic Categories

We can divide the main problems of cybernetics into three classes as follows:

1. To construct an effective theory, with or without hardware models to represent the theory, such that artificial intelligence can be manufactured. This is the problem of **synthesis**, and pays no attention to the means of the achievement.

2. To produce models and theories of human behaviour, which present these functions of human beings, and other systems, in much the same manner as they are performed by human beings. In other words, it is not enough merely to produce the same end result, but to produce the same result by similar, or even identical, means. This is the problem of **simulation**.

3. Finally, to reproduce, either by synthesis or by simulation, the whole of human (or animal) behaviour by models which are identical in their construction with human beings or animals. That is, they should in the end be chemical-colloidal (protoplasmic) systems.

To take the last class of problems first, it would certainly seem that we are far from being able to tackle them at present. Indeed, so little has been done to build 'protoplasmic' systems directly that we can soon pass on to the first two, more realistic, categories. In the third category of problems we might include those cases of building artificial internal organs, which may ultimately be used to replace human organs which, for one reason or another, have failed.

At this stage, most artificial organs come in the second category, since they are obviously not made of the same materials as those used in the construction of human beings. An iron lung, for example, may perform a similar function to a human lung, but still does not perform the function in the same way; instead of placing the iron lung inside the body, the body is placed inside the iron lung. There are, however, some artificial internal organs which do come much nearer to construction in the same way as the original body organs. A few models have already been suggested, and some actually built; some are basically chemical, or physico-chemical, or even colloidal in their construction, and are, therefore, part of our third category of cybernetic problems.

As is often the case with cybernetic research, a great many practical offshoots emerge from origins which had other goals. In the case of chemical models, the development of a chemical storage system for computers is an off-shoot of considerable commercial importance. By and large, however, the third category of cybernetic problems is very much in the future. This is not to say that this third category will not ultimately become the most important of the three; but it is one that is bound to depend on development and research in the first two, as well as in the various relevant branches of chemistry and physics.

We shall argue that there is no reason to doubt the *possibility* of constructing a human being artificially, and we must assume that, at some stage, cybernetic research will be concerned with just this.

Let us look next at the first category of cybernetic problems, because it is from this that the main applications of cybernetics emanate in the form of automation. Here we can construct models of the following types:

1. Finite automata.
2. Infinite automata.
3. Information theoretic models.
4. Probability theory models, statistical and other mathematic models.

5. Computer programs.

6. Servo-systems.

7. Any models whatever, in any fabric (hardware) hatever, other than those which are in our third category of cybernetic problems.

These same methods apply, of course, to the second ategory of cybernetic problems, where we reproduce the ame end results, simulating human behaviour, by imilar means. Here, as far as biology is concerned, we hall be especially interested in models of the special enses (eyes, ears, etc.) and in models of cognition, specially learning, motivation, perception, memory, hinking and language, as well as in genetics, and the entral nervous system.

Many of these cybernetic methods or approaches to ybernetics will be discussed in this book. We shall escribe, in outline, digital computers and their programming, as well as information theory. We shall also iscuss logic briefly. Logic is relevant to computers and s also the basis of a particular class of finite automata alled neural nets. These automata attempt to simulate, lirectly, the human nervous system and are very closely elated to developments in logic; hence a certain minimum knowledge of logic is a basic essential.

In Cybernetics we are especially interested in the class f finite automata which learn from experience or adapt o changing circumstances. A finite automaton is a ystem constructed according to certain specific rules and omposed of a finite number of elements; each of the lements is capable of being in only one of a finite number of possible states at any particular time. The model, r automaton, has an input and an output and a store for nformation. We are concerned to choose our models vith the specific intention of simulating biological and ehavioural systems. We can think of our model as a ollection of inter-connected cells, or we can think of it as

a tape-machine. A tape-machine has a tape of any num
ber of rows, which can be thought of as being ruled o
into squares; the tape passes under a device which scan
one or more squares at a time. The tape may mov
backwards or forwards underneath the scanner accord
ing to specific rules which might collectively be called th
program of the taped automaton. This has the effect o
controlling the automaton's activity in much the sam
way as a computer program controls a computer'
activity.

Digital computers, *tape automata* and *logical o
neural* nets are, in fact, much the same as each other i
their capability.

At this stage it should be clear to the reader that we ar
dealing with a form of model which is *diminishing th
distinction* which we normally make between 'softwar
(e.g. theories and programs) and 'hardware' (e.g. serv
systems and computers). This is precisely what is require
for an effective theory; we know it does a job, and w
know it from a description of the system without buildin
it. We want a blueprint, and for many purposes this wi
be as useful as the machine actually being made. By
blueprint, we mean something which is so precise tha
from it a machine could most certainly be made; it is, a
we would say, effective. Even blueprints, under certai
circumstances, may omit bits and pieces, but this doe
not make them useless. Axiomatic systems, as we hav
already said, are important examples of such blueprint

We shall try in this book to add detail to the gener
arguments and descriptions of both this and the firs
chapter. We shall throughout be concerned primaril
with views about artificial intelligence and the simulatio
of human behaviour; this is what cybernetics is abou
The remainder of this book is a development in detail c
this second chapter, together with the more gener
picture of the first.

SUMMARY
This chapter has discussed self-adapting systems and draws attention to the various categories of such self-adapting systems.

Models and theories, in the form of automata, neural nets, mathematical and statistical theories, information theoretic models and others, all form part of the subject matter of cybernetics.

The three main categories of cybernetic problem are described, and the importance of model-making to each category is made clear.

CHAPTER THREE

THE DEVELOPMENT OF CYBERNETIC MODELS

ARGUMENT

Many models have been built in hardware to demonstrate organismic behaviour. Surprising as it may seem at first sight, most people are more impressed by simulations of human behaviour entailing actual physical movement by some piece of hardware than they are by the most complicated of theories. This is so, even though systems like computers, which do not actually move, perform operations which are far more sophisticated than the most complex of the maze-running type of automata.

The simplest sort of organismic system is one that illustrates *tropistic* capacities, where tropisms are simple innate responses to features of the environment. So a machine which follows a light source, or will learn to run away from a light source or some other stimulus, tends by the very nature of things to look more like a living creature than a computer which, for all its complexity of structure and intricacy of detail, lacks the visual appeal.

The idea of 'man as a machine' has long stimulated people to talk and think in terms of robots, or automata, and this in turn has stimulated the manufacture of electrical, mechanical, chemical or other models which may be manufactured by any means whatever. These models are either of 'whole organisms', of special parts of organisms such as eyes and ears, or they are attempts to show some of the principles which are used in the field of human intelligence. The eventual aim may be to build a human being artificially, but such an aim must still be a long way off. This, though, is what is needed—a functional blueprint for a human being.

The whole thing varies from toys to complex equipment of great practical value, at least in application.

One aspect of cybernetics is the process of model construction in hardware; it is this we shall take up in this chapter.

Scientists have always constructed models, and insofar as such models are often helpful both for demonstration purposes and for the clarification of the scientist's own ideas, it is obviously an area which should be encouraged.

Cybernetic development in recent years has made a move gradually away from hardware to software models. The reason for this is the difficulty of building a sufficiently large and instructive hardware model with the limited time the scientist has and the amount of money available. It is for this reason that computers, which can be suitably programmed, have taken preference over the development of hardware models. In using the term 'hardware' here we are not, of course, referring to computer hardware, but to special purpose hardware models.

As we have said, the advantage of the hardware model is that it has a persuasive force and an appeal to the human eye which no computer or purely theoretical model can ever have. Therefore it is not surprising to find that a number of 'special purpose' hardware models have been built over the years. We shall describe a few selected examples with a view to clarifying the general process of hardware modelling. The processes modelled are often quite simple, so the reader need have no apprehensions about handling too much technical detail.

The models deal with movement, towards light or in running a maze, and the principles by which information is sensed (equivalent of seen or heard) and processed inside the mechanism itself (the brain). These principles, while simply demonstrated, could, especially when combined, be of the utmost importance to our understanding of how the brain works.

Grey Walter's Models

Dr. Grey Walter of the Burden Neurological Institute produced two of the first cybernetic models. He built a simple conditioned reflex analogue model, called **Cora**; he also built a machine, which is popularly known as a 'tortoise', capable of moving around and imitating the automatic (tropistic) act of following a light source.

Cora is a very simple type of conditioned reflex machine; its response unit is a neon tube which flashes when it responds to a particular stimulus. If a whistle is sounded as a sign of a forthcoming light stimulus, then **Cora** will flash in response to the whistle—whereas originally it responded only to the flash of light. This simply illustrates the association necessary to simple conditioning: the sort of conditioning we have come to associate with Pavlov's dogs.

The tortoise is a fairly complicated system, with two sensory elements which take the form of a simple contact receptor and a photo-electric cell. The tortoise is in a frame, rather like a Link Trainer plotter ('crab'), which moves around the floor and is driven by an electric motor. It carries an accumulator on its chassis, two valves, registers, condensers and a pilot light. The behaviour of the tortoise is simply tropistic because it follows a light source. It differs from the Link Trainer plotter as it has no link cable to a power or information source.

Uttley's Models

Professor A. M. Uttley has built two hardware models, one of which is the classification model and the other the conditional probability model. These are rather different from Grey Walter's models as they are strictly passive and lack mobility, and were built to illustrate the basic principles of classification and conditional probability.

The principle of classification is thought by many

people to be basic to conception, involving a number of different stimulus units which can classify an input as it occurs. If one has an input, to take the simplest example, made of three input elements, a, b and c, either they all fire or some of them fire. So we may say an object which fires all of a, b and c is one sort of object, an object which fires a and b alone is another sort, an object that fires a and c alone is another sort and so on.

A complete classification system provides for every possible set of combinations of the input elements. This means that for inputs a, b, c and d we have outputs a, b, c and d, ab, ac, ad, bc, bd, cd, abc, abd, bcd, acd and $abcd$. We can think of a, b, c and d as colours, shapes, sizes, etc., and we can reconstruct by such means all the objects we see in our environment.

But there are reasons for doubting that such an overall classificatory method is suitable as a model of the human sensory system because of its enormous size and because we should have many legitimate combinations which are never met in real life. There is, however, a close resemblance in principle, and one that demands the most detailed attention.

Uttley's second model is based on his idea that suggests that, if a record is kept of present and past events, then predictions can be made about future occurrences.

For example, if we say that A is followed by B on every single occasion, then we can write the probability of B following A, i.e. $\mathbf{P}(B/A)=1$, which is another way of saying that B will *always* follow A. Such a sequence of events is not necessarily 'certain', since, although it has always occurred that way in the experience of the system computing, there is no guarantee that it will not change in the future. In the same way the probability of one event following another can be recorded and an estimate given of the chances of some event X, say, following some other event Y. It may happen any part of the time from

0 (=never) to 1 (=always), and when it does it is measured by some fraction lying between 0 and 1, and possibly including 0 and 1.

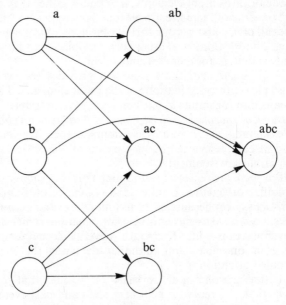

Figure 1
*Input elements a, b and c are classed completely into all their
possible combinations ab, ac, bc and abc.*

Conditional probability, as we call this notion of
dependent occurrences, obviously bears some relationship to the way human beings store and utilize information for predictive purposes. To this extent Uttley, in
building his own conditional probability machine, was
simulating a very important aspect of idealized human
behaviour. Figure 1 shows the basic principle of complete
classification.

Uttley's model throws up some difficulties. Both classification and conditional probability systems can be conjoined to make one large model; the problem arises when we try to generalize to show how all of human behaviour, and perhaps also all the structural features of the nervous system, accommodate this sort of modelling. The truth is that we have to weigh so many different features of this conditional probability model that it is difficult to be sure that the original principle is still really utilized in the model in any important sense.

There still remains evidence that the conditional probability and the classification method is basic to artificial intelligence. What we have to accept is that the conditional probabilities become a very much more complicated matter than merely recording one event following another, or two or more events either following each other or occurring together. Such events have to be recorded, but in a hierarchical order. Therefore one event may be said to follow another event at one level of description—say at the level of an external act like eating —whereas this implies the most detailed analysis of a complex of events following a complex of events at a more detailed level. It is therefore at a different level— say, at the level of the activity of the nervous system which accompanies eating.

It is not only that the ability to describe an artificially intelligent system demands treatment on many different levels of description, but also that many events are related to other events in a complicated fashion, all of which the human brain is capable of processing. We may expect certain events, A, to happen if B happens and if and only if C happened before B. This example is meant to illustrate the more complicated conditions which will pertain in many cases. Not only that, but there will be changing circumstances, which make even a complete record of the past unsatisfactory in estimating what is likely to happen in the immediate future. Uttley recognised this in his conditional probability model and weighted probabilities in terms of *recency*. The difficulty here is that recency is far from being the only factor affecting probability considerations in the making of immediate decisions. Perhaps the biggest difficulty for Uttley's systems is that a clear-cut distinction is not made between symbols and the things that symbols denote.

In an intelligent automaton we have to distinguish sharply between linguistic considerations and so called 'factual' considerations. A failure to recognise this distinction is a failure to recognise the full range of artificial intelligence. It is no criticism of Uttley that his models have not, as yet, been taken to this next stage, which is extremely difficult to achieve, but a recent paper of his attempts to bring his original models into line with the facts by cutting down on his complete classification system.

A further factor which should be mentioned at this point is that any model of the human intelligence, even at its more lowly levels, is liable ultimately to be statistical rather than deterministic. By this we mean that the complexities of the world as such, and the way it processes these complexities, are almost certainly best described on a statistical rather than a precise deterministic basis. In other words, complete precision, derived by a one-to-one contact of elements or neurones in the nervous system, is unlikely to be a realistic modelling. This may be taken by some readers to mean that the whole concept of a deterministic model is wrong and that we should have approached the matter statistically in the first place. Whether or not this is so, the reason for approaching it in a deterministic fashion is that it is then easier to see the logic of the situation clearly depicted. When we have these principles clear we can consider how best to provide the necessary statistical descriptions.

The Homeostat

Professor Ross Ashby's best known model is **The Homeostat**. This is a machine designed to illustrate the principle of what he calls ultra-stability; this is a really stable state where no further goal-seeking occurs. The Homeostat is not a moving machine and is built primarily to illustrate a principle, rather than to demonstrate the outward show of organismic type behaviour.

The Homeostat consists of four boxes with magnetic needle pivots on the top of each; the needles can be deflected from their normal neutral positions after which they can return to the position of equilibrium. The main feature of this homeostatically controlled system is that the return of the needles to the neutral position can vary as a function of the circumstances in which the original deflection took place.

Pask's Models

Professor Gordon Pask has built a whole series of hardware models and automata, representing different aspects of organismic structure and function. Many of these have been concerned with teaching on a group basis, or learning on both an individual and a group basis; he has always been concerned with different aspects of self-adaptation and the evolution of systems in an environment. The notion of a system, model or organism evolving is very similar to that of its learning and adapting to the environment.

Perhaps the best known of the many models suggested and built by Professor Pask is the one showing the growth of threads in an electro-magnetic field. The threads can be seen as they grow and develop, breaking and regenerating themselves as the field potentials change. The idea is that there is an actual growth process; the threads can go back to solution or be re-formed as threads, making the most complicated patterns, as a function not only of their own state of the time of their regeneration, but also of the distribution of the electro-magnetic field. This clearly is the type of model which attempts to simulate the growth aspects of organisms from a cybernetic point of view. Mackay and Ainsworth have produced somewhat similar models for simulating the growth aspect of an organismic process; indeed it is believed that these have prior claims. But from our point of view they illustrate much the same principle, referred to by Pask as illustrative of the development of a concept at the neural level.

For Running Mazes

Many different kinds of models have been built to illustrate the learning of mazes and we shall not attempt to discuss any individual one here. We shall merely mention that among the best known ones are those built by Wiener, Shannon and Deutsch. All of these maze running models were based on essentially the same principle of simple **selective reinforcement**. It is easy enough to see that if you have a model which can record that it is blocked or not blocked at a 'choice point' in a maze, and can retain this fact, then the next time through the maze, instead of going to the turning blocked (if it is a two-choice point), it goes to one that is open. Learning in this somewhat simple sense is a fairly obvious feature. Consider the following maze:

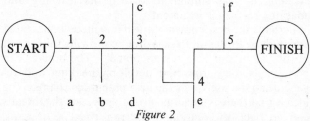

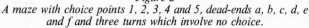

Figure 2
A maze with choice points 1, 2, 3, 4 and 5, dead-ends a, b, c, d, e and f and three turns which involve no choice.

It will be seen that, at choice point **1**, if the model goes right the first time it is blocked at *a*, it records the fact, and has to return; it then has the choice of right or left at **1**. If it goes left it goes back to the beginning where it has to turn round—but it then has no choice point with a *new* branch to go up again. At the point **1** it would go straight on rather than right since the right path at *a* is known to be blocked. The second choice procedure at *b* is the same as the first. The third choice point, at *c*, is a three choice point. The model might make two mistakes before it learns to go the correct way; and so on through the maze until the end is reached. It need hardly be added that this represents no complicated logical principle. It is simply a matter of deciding how to store the information and how the interaction between the machine and the outside world should be achieved. It is usually achieved by some simple sensing device, such as a photo-electric cell or selenium disc. The store itself contains the beginnings of a simple model of its environment, in this case the maze; but the principle of internal modelling is quite general.

Maze running machines have the advantage of illustrating clearly the simplicity of some simple learning processes. On the other hand one difficulty is that, having gone so far in the correct, and certainly the most dramatic direction, there is a limit to the actual effectiveness of the process, when the need arises to generalize on them and to show more complex learning. This could be achieved if the maze-runner has the capacity, say, either to burrow under or to climb over the walls of the maze.

Growth Classification Models

Chapman's system—which is a form of growth model—differs from Uttley's in that it grows, is not pre-wired and does not require *complete* classification. It demands that any number of elements can be gathered together into several of the *possible* sets of combinations of their elements. There is the further condition that the several combinations of elements which can be gathered together shall be those which occur most frequently.

At first sight the limitation on the number of combinations which can be classified appears to be a simplification imposing an unjustifiable limitation on the system. However, if we consider a situation similar to that of visual perception, where the number of elements is so large that only a tiny fraction of the possible number of combinations occurs, the economy of Chapman's system becomes obvious. The condition of relating priority of classification to frequency of occurrence inevitably means that the system does not classify elements immediately, and at this stage is therefore perhaps not strictly a classifying system. Its structure is such that, by operating on it with groups of elements, it 'grows' and *learns* to classify them. Chapman's system learns to classify; Uttley's system classifies to learn.

The technique by which this is achieved in the hardware model is 'inhibition'. Each input to the machine represents an element, or primitive stimulus, and is connected to every one of the outputs, representing events, by a number of barely conducting paths consisting of threads of cotton moistened with lime water. Then with firing, threads become more sensitive and, by implication, those fired less often become less sensitive. Figure 3 shows the principle of partial and partitioned classification, as well as inhibition. By partitioned, we mean the sub-classification of inputs prior to higher level classification.

Partitioned classification could apply to combining what we see with what we hear; it could apply to either Uttley's or Chapman's models.

Chapman's model is significant in itself as a pointer to the way in which economy can be achieved in a large

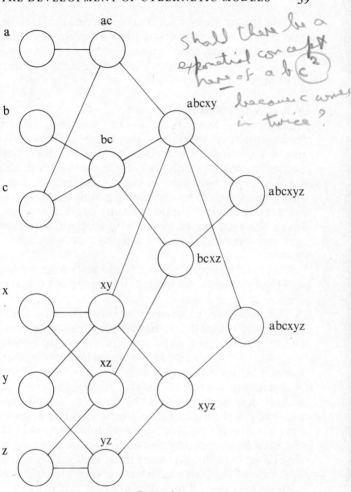

Shall there be a exponential concept here of a b c ? because c comes in twice ?

Figure 3
Shows two basic sets of inputs a, b, c and x, y, z; they overlap at later points such as bcxz. They are initially partitioned *and are clearly in the case of a, b, c-set incomplete.*

classification system; what is more important is that he, like Pask, has demonstrated that a highly organized specific system can grow in a non-specific medium with a relatively simple structure while obeying certain general rules of growth.

Neural Net Models in Hardware

These models, built by the author, were built directly from neural net descriptions (see Chapter 5). The first model shows a particular classification and conditional probability system. Only two inputs are classified, and the memory is only over six events, but the model can easily be extended, by the use of additional relays, to include any number of inputs and any length of memory. It can also be extended to deal with temporal sequences and any form of association whatever between the inputs.

This brief statement applies to the first of the models and Figure 4 shows the principle in simple block diagram form.

The second model was built in hardware units whose memory has now been extended to something near eighty events. There were some twelve of these units available, and they could be connected in any way whatever to realize a wide variety of different automata. These automata are capable of realizing all the characteristics already described, and could be shown to demonstrate many of the characteristics of simple learning. Some of the units could be regarded as motivation units, and thus the effectiveness of any association may be made to depend on their firing at some time. Figure 20 (Chapter 8) illustrates this principle in terms of neural nets, where each element has a threshold number.

It is difficult to draw conclusions from what we have said about hardware models. But we ought, perhaps, to remind the reader that we have selected just a few illustrative models which are generally fairly simple and concerned with illustrating principles which are thought to play an important part in the organization of the human brain and nervous system.

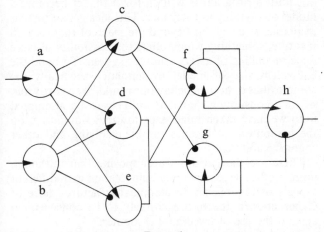

Figure 4

Shows elements a, b, . . ., h, where a and b are inputs, and where circular (filled-in) endings are stopping pulses and filled-in arrows are starting pulses: so if a and b fire together d and c will not fire, but c will. f and g have feedback loops which cause them to re-member. So a and b firing together will be recalled at f and this sends a memory pulse to f.

Others, such as Goldacre, Harman, Minsky, Selfridge, together with many other well-known cyberneticians, have also built models which illustrate different aspects of human or organismic growth development and intelligence, but space forbids us to show any more examples.

What is clear, above all else, is the need for larger scale models, capable of depicting more complex systems which combine classification, conditional probabilities, stability-seeking and the like. This suggests the use of the large scale digital computer and the reasons for this are fairly simple. A computer may cost more than a million pounds to build and is universal, in the sense that it is not until a program is written for it that it becomes a model of anything in particular. This means that there is available, at a cost far beyond the reach of the research institute, something which offers the possibility of large scale modelling of a very complex system. To build the equivalent size of model to simulate specifically the complexities of human behaviour would be so costly and so time consuming that it is unlikely to be attempted until we have taken huge steps towards simulating, on the computer, intelligence, problem-solving and other cognitive abilities.

These are the reasons for supposing that, although more models were inevitably built dealing with different aspects of organismic development structure, more of Cybernetics in the future is likely to be concentrated around the use of the digital computer.

Figure 5 shows the relation of such special purpose models to the bulk of cybernetics.

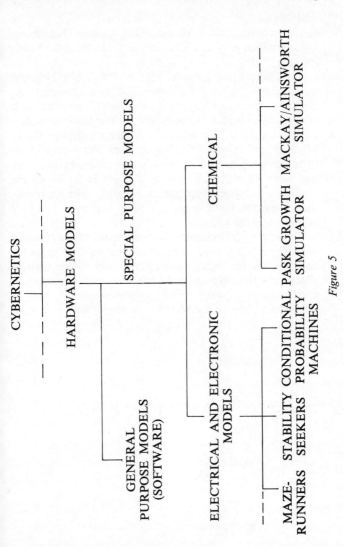

Figure 5

SUMMARY

In this chapter we have described various 'hardware' models which may be collected together under the heading of cybernetics.

In particular we have referred to the Ashby Homeostat, Grey Walter's tortoises, Uttley's classification machine and conditional probability machine, and Chapman's classification machine. We have also discussed briefly the chemical hardware models of Pask, Mackay and Ainsworth. Wiener and Shannon's maze running machine and Deutsch's maze running machine are taken as representative of this group of hardware models and were described collectively. We then discussed partial, partitioned and adaptive (growth) types of classification models.

The aim of this chapter is to illustrate, by selecting a few of the better known hardware models, the type of construction that has gone on in the field of cybernetics, which is primarily to make clear to the student the achievements of cybernetics on the one hand, and to clarify the ideas of the scientist on the other.

CHAPTER FOUR
LOGIC AND AUTOMATA THEORY

ARGUMENT

This chapter is about logic and automata. Automata can occur either in hardware or software, although we tend to think of the theory of automata as very much a software approach to the subject. Here, in contrast to the last chapter, we are thinking of software methods.

We have both finite and infinite automata. Infinite (or non-finite) automata tend to be associated especially with **Turing machines** and the foundations of classical mathematics.

Logic and the development of decision procedures (algorithms) are closely associated with the concept of an automaton. It is indeed essential to understand some part of the development of modern symbolic logic to appreciate fully the development of automata theory. The development of symbolic logic is bound up with the field of metamathematics—which is concerned with the analysis of the basis on which mathematics is constructed—and Boolean algebra, which is the field of the application of algebra to logic whose origin has always been closely associated with the Irish mathematician George Boole.

Automata theory and symbolic logic are cornerstones of cybernetic development, for they emphasise the important fact that the *effectiveness* of theories (their ability to formulate a theory which we know can lead to an actual construction) is what is required. This is what we have previously described as the search for a blueprint.

'Robot' (or 'automaton') is a word often used to apply to artificial, usually imaginary, human beings. It applies to one of the most important types of model used by cyberneticians trying to simulate the function and structure of the human being. This is one of the aims of the set of models called finite automata.

Finite automata may be variously defined, but can best be described as systems constructed according to certain rules such that the systems may take on only a finite number of different states. One way we can conceive of them is as paper tape machines, as was mentioned in an earlier chapter. We can think of a tape as being ruled off into squares and placed on rollers moving backwards and forwards, or perhaps in one direction only, beneath a scanner. Turing machines are tape automata of the two-way kind, i.e. they may move backwards or forwards under the scanner.

But let us look more carefully at **logic** before we discuss automata further, since it is from logic that the idea of artificial intelligence systems springs.

Logic

We shall try now to develop formal logic, as it is sometimes called. The reason the word 'formal' is used is because certain logical relationships, such as the relationship of inference from one statement to another, depends on the *formal* relationship which exists between those statements. For example, if I say 'Rhoda is the sister of Clara', then I am saying something about a relationship between two people or even between two things, so that I could say 'X is to the left of Y', or 'Harry is married to Anne'. These are relational statements and we could say that the relation between two people could be represented by some letter such as R and the two people by any two letters such as x and y.

If we transcribe such statements into symbolic form—
a sort of code—we have Rxy; for it does not matter what
we replace x and y by, or whom we replace x and y by. We
are saying that there is a certain relationship between two
people or things and this has a form which does not
depend upon the particular nature of the things; it is
entirely dependent upon the nature of the relationship.

If we take one specific relation like 'to the right of' and
say 'Harry is to the right of Bill' or 'Jill is to the right of
Jack', then in both cases the sentences do not depend
upon who the particular people are. The important point
is simply that a certain relationship, 'to the right of', is
independent of the particular items named.

This brings out, quite typically, the point about the
'formal' nature of logic. We shall now try to develop a
part of formal logic: where formal logic applies to the
sentences) from a linguistic background. The form is
axiomatic, in effect, and the origins lie in ordinary
linguistic usage.

In describing logic we use the words 'term' and 'proposition' very frequently. The word 'term' is equivalent
to the word 'class'; i.e. a 'term' is the name for some class
of objects, while 'proposition' means communication by
a sentence. It is something like, say, 'Charlie is Dad's
brother'.

We must remind ourselves that sentences or statements
in English are generally capable of being split up into
subject and predicate. The subject represents a 'term' and
the predicate, which may represent a 'term', will also
involve a relational statement, which is a verb, and may,
of course, include all sorts of connectives such as 'and',
'or' etc. One of the principal logical forms which has been
fairly systematically investigated is the **syllogism**. The
syllogism is a form of argument where a direct inference
is made from two propositions to a third proposition.
The first two propositions are rather like axioms, but

the third proposition, which is the conclusion, is rather like a theorem.

The propositions which make up the syllogism are all of the form:

> 'All S is P'
> 'No S is P'
> 'Some S is P'
> 'Some S is not P'

Or to give more concrete particular examples:

> 'All women are wise'
> 'No woman is foolish'
> 'Some women are foolish'
> 'Some women are not wise'

We will now put different propositions (three at a time) of these four types together, to form an argument of the kind:

> If a and b, then c.

Let us give an example:

> If 'All women are wise'
> and 'Jacqueline is a woman'
> then 'Jacqueline is wise'.

This is a syllogistic form of argument which allows the deduction of a conclusion from a major and minor premise. The premises we have referred to are the axioms of the system.

Propositions, or statements as we sometimes call them, expressed as sentences in English, have a subject and a predicate. So that in the statement 'All women are wise', we say that 'All women' is the subject and 'are wise' is the predicate. To understand the syllogistic form of argument more completely, we must now define the rather difficult concept of *distribution*. The reader who wishes to understand the logic of the syllogism should spend some time on this concept.

A subject is said to be distributed if it refers to *all* the members of some class of objects or people. We use the word 'term' to refer to the name of some class of objects, people, and then ask if it is distributed; does the statement apply to *all* members of the class? For example, in the statement 'All women are wise', 'women' (the subject) is clearly distributed because it refers to the class of all women, whereas the predicate 'are wise' is not distributed because it can refer to men, children, perhaps even to horses, cats or dogs.

Undistributed means 'not universally applicable' and distributed means the opposite. To understand deductive arguments in syllogistic form, it is essential, we must repeat, to understand the notion of distribution. It is also vital to understand the notion of 'term'. In the statement 'All women are wise', 'women' and 'wise' are both terms. In the statement 'Some cats are good-tempered', 'cats' and 'good-tempered' are both terms. Terms are words defining a class of objects or people.

Remember that a subject or predicate which is *distributed* refers to the *whole* of a class, or to the whole of whatever the relevant term refers. We can now look again at our general forms of statement acceptable to syllogism:

'All S is P'

'No S is P'

'Some S is P'

'Some S is not P'

We classify these general forms as having distributed subjects and predicates. So the following table applies:

Proposition	Subject	Predicate
All S is P	distributed	undistributed
No S is P	distributed	distributed
Some S is P	undistributed	undistributed
Some S is not P	undistributed	distributed

We say that '*some* or *anything*' is always undistributed and that when either the *S* or the *P* (i.e. subject or predicate) is negative then the predicate is always distributed. Now, armed with this information, we can look at the *valid forms* and *moods* of the syllogism, remembering that all syllogisms are of the form:

If *a* and *b*, then *c*

where *a*, *b* and *c* are statements that may take any of the four above forms.

Prior to stating these rules we must notice the use of the words 'middle term'.

'If Tours is in France
and I am in Tours,
then I am in France.'

This is clearly a deductive argument in syllogistic form, and the term occurring in both the major and minor premises, but *not* in the conclusion, is called the 'middle term'.

We should note that by 'general' statements we mean statements starting with 'all' or 'no'; by 'particular' statements we mean statements starting with 'some'.

Now we will list the rules for valid syllogisms:

1. In a syllogism, the middle term must be distributed once at least.

2. No term must be distributed in the conclusion if it was not distributed in one of the premises.

3. You cannot make an inference from two negative premises or from two 'particular' premises.

4. If one premise is negative (or particular), the conclusion must be negative (or particular), and vice-versa. These four rules eliminate possible combinations of statements which would otherwise make up valid syllogisms. This means that we cannot permit as valid syllogistic forms such as:

'If I am not in Tours and if Tours is
not in France, then . . .'

It can easily be seen that no conclusion can be drawn from these two premises. We shall not attempt to show which syllogisms are valid moods, but clearly the ones we have already used such as:

> 'If Tours is in France
> and I am in Tours,
> then I am in France.'

are valid because they do not offend against any one of our four rules of validity.

We have one further consideration to bear in mind before we are eventually left with only valid syllogisms. The last consideration is about *Figures*; and Figures further restrict the range of possible moods.

Syllogisms are deductive arguments involving three statements and each statement involves two terms. So a syllogism is of the form YX, ZY, ZX where Y is the middle term. But this is not the only form. We can supply a simple table, where Y is always the middle term, i.e.:

	I	II	III	IV
Major Premise	YX	XY	YX	XY
Minor Premise	ZY	ZY	YZ	YZ
Conclusion	ZX	ZX	ZX	ZX

All valid moods must also be capable of inclusion in the form of this table of figures.

There is a further restriction; 5 of the 24 possible valid moods which can be put into these figures, are *weak* arguments. This means that they may be of the form:

> 'If all Dutch are clever, and all
> clever people are blue-eyed,
> then some Dutch are blue-eyed.'

This is obviously weak, because we could have inferred that all Dutch are blue-eyed.

We shall say no more about this form of argument, although the reader might be interested in personally working out the remaining 19 valid syllogistic moods and figures.

We shall turn next to a brief discussion of logic which takes a more mathematical, or symbolic, form. We shall outline the basic principles of *Boolean Algebra*—the 'calculus of classes' as it is sometimes called. Having already indicated that a term usually refers to a class of some sort, we shall say now that any well-defined collection of objects is a set or class. We can thus talk of the class of all blue and all yellow objects, the class of snakes, of all cobras, of all cylindrical objects and so on. We can represent a class by a circle, and for convenience represent the whole universe of all possible classes by a rectangle.

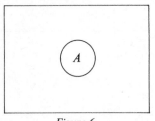

Figure 6

Figure 6 represents a class of objects A, and this may, of course, be any set of objects of any colour, shape or property.

If we now call the complete universe of all possible classes by the number 1, we can then say that everything that is not A (represented by A') and everything that is A make up the whole of the universe.

$$A \cdot A' = 1$$

where '.' means *and* and the prime sign (') means *not*. So if we think of *A* as 'all blue objects' and *A'* as 'everything that is not blue', we are absolutely right. We assume of course that everything in the world can be described as blue or not-blue; we resolve every doubt by such conventions as are necessary. We assume here a well-defined boundary between classes of objects.

If we add next a second class, *B*, we may find any one of four relations existing between *A* and *B*; these relations can be represented by any of the four following diagrams:

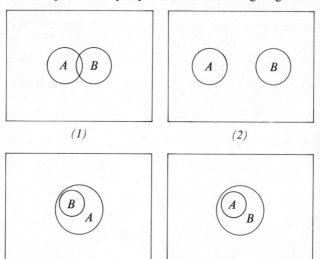

(1)   (2)

(3)   (4)

Figure 7

The diagrams we have just used to represent our classes and their relations are called Euler-Venn diagrams. They represent classes named *A*, *B*, *C* . . . as areas contained within circles.

In Figure 7(1), *A* and *B* overlap; in Figure 7(2) *A* and *B* do not overlap, while in the other two cases either A is contained in B, or vice-versa.

If we define the value 1 as representing the set of all possible classes and the value 0 as being the null set (the class with no members), then we can write $A \cap B$ for 'the overlap of A and B'. So

$$A \cap B \neq 0 \qquad . \qquad . \qquad . \qquad (1)$$

means 'A and B overlap' and

$$A \cap B = 0 \qquad . \qquad . \qquad . \qquad (2)$$

means 'A and B do not overlap'.

(1) may represent some such statement as, 'Some objects are both blue and square at the same time' and

(2) represents such statements as 'No object can be both circular and square at the same time'.

The other two Euler-Venn diagrams of Figure 7 show A contained in B, and vice-versa. We write these:

$$A \subset B = A \cap B = B . \qquad . \qquad . \qquad (3)$$

and

$$B \subset A = B \cap A = A . \qquad . \qquad . \qquad (4)$$

respectively, where the symbol '$\subset$' means 'is contained in'.

Now we can build up other logical relations involving either 'and' or 'or', where we define 'and' and 'or' as follows:

$$A \cdot B \qquad . \qquad . \qquad . \qquad (5)$$

means 'A and B'

and $\qquad\qquad A \text{ v } B \qquad . \qquad . \qquad . \qquad (6)$

means 'A or B or both', so that $A \text{ v } B = 1$ is represented in the same way as

$$A \cup B = 1$$

where $\cup$ means the same as **v** and represents 'inclusive or'.

And if $A \cdot B = 1$, then it is the same as $A \cap B = 1$.
We can represent these logical formulae in what are
sometimes called truth-tables.

The truth-table for 'not' (') is:

A	A'
0	1
1	0

For 'and' (.):

A	B	$A \cdot B$
1	0	0
0	1	0
1	1	1
0	0	0

And for 'or' (v) it is:

A	B	$A \vee B$
1	0	1
0	1	1
1	1	1
0	0	0

We can combine the truth tables for **v** and ' (or and not) to define a new connective of 'material implication'. By material implication we mean that some statements materially imply some other statements. This is intended to mean something like 'If I am king of Siam then I am royal' but in practice the two propositions connected by material implication need not, in the formal system, be connected in any causal sense. The general form taken is 'If . . . then . . .' and we must formalise this.

We say:

$$A \supset B = \text{df} \ A' \, \mathbf{v} \, B \quad . \quad . \quad . \quad (7)$$

where 'df' means 'by definition'. We say that A implies B means that: it is not the case that A, or B, where, of course, not A is written A'. We write the truth-table as follows:

A'	B	$A \supset B$
1	0	0
0	1	1
1	1	1
0	0	1

The reader should try to derive this truth-table for himself by combining the truth-table of **v** and ' as given in (7).

The combination of A and B to give $A \supset B$ is easily understood from the definition of $A \supset B = A' \, \mathbf{v} \, B$. We need the truth-table for $A \, \mathbf{v} \, B$, in which, instead of A we substitute A'.

Finally we can state a postulate set, such as:

For any classes $A, B, C, \ldots, 1, 0$ belonging to a Boolean algebra $\mathbf{B}^*$, in which 1 is the universal class and 0 is the null class:

1. A, B are classes belonging to $\mathbf{B}^*$, and $A \cap B$ is a class belonging to $\mathbf{B}^*$. This is written $A, B\varepsilon\mathbf{B}^*$ and $(A \cap B) \in \mathbf{B}^*$, where $\in$ means 'belonging to'.

2. $A, B \varepsilon \mathbf{B}^*$ and also $(A \cup B) \varepsilon \mathbf{B}^*$.

3. $A \cap 0 = A = 0 \cap A$.

4. $A \cup 1 = 1 = 1 \cup A$.

5. $A \cap B = B \cap A$.

6. $A \cup B = B \cup A$.

7. $A \cup (B \cap C) = (A \cup B) \cap (A \cup C)$.

8. $A \cap (B \cup C) = (A \cap B) \cup (A \cap C)$.

9. $A \cap A' = 0$.

10. $A \cup A' = 1$.

11. A Boolean Algebra $\mathbf{B}^*$ is composed of at least two classes A and B from which theorems in Boolean Algebra about any number of classes may be derived.

We shall do no more here than introduce these basic statements about logic, except to add that we can, if we so desire, interpret the classes $A, B, \ldots, N$ as propositions $p, q, \ldots, w$. This means instead of relationships between classes of things (or their names) we have relations between propositions, which we can think of as being expressed by sentences. We now change the values 0 and 1 to **f** and **t**, which stand respectively for falsehood and truth.

We can, of course, formulate other systems of logic, such as many-valued logic which does not limit itself to the values 0 and 1. If we consider all the real numbers in the interval $(0,1)$ we could interpret these values as probabilities. We can also define operators or relations needed to produce and enrich our precise language. An operator is something like a connective or a verb in ordinary language. A relation is like an operator of the kind '. . . is a brother of . . .' and is basically the same as an operator.

As far as cybernetics is concerned logic plays a very important part. It has the necessary precision and clearly bears some relation to the way people, or certainly machines, 'think'. A computer operates on a logical basis and models of behaviour can be described in logical terms—whether that logic be of a precise or probabilistic form. Language, too, can be reconstructed in terms of such a symbolic logic.

Introducing Finite Automata

What we have said about logic leads naturally to a discussion of automata; a Boolean Algebra, such as **B***, is capable of being described in terms of an algorithm and an algorithm (precise decision procedure) is, in effect, an automaton. Perhaps it would be better to call it a blueprint for a hardware automaton.

We think of automata as tape machines, as already discussed. We can think of the automata as ruled into squares, having symbols in each square. The automaton scans each square one at a time and as a result we say it generates theorems, performs computations or solves problems.

The field of automata theory has now a long and important history. Such methods were used to prove theorems about the formation of mathematics and lie at the foundation of what is known to be *computable*.

In recent years we have come to consider automata with many different tapes, either moving together or moving separately, with tapes that go both left to right and right to left, or tapes that go one way only. Figure 8 shows a Turing Machine where the tape is wound on two spools.

Let us show a simple example of a Turing Machine type of computation. We will suppose that on the tape is the following ordered set of symbols

                    011111101110

Let us further suppose that it contains the following instructions:

1. At first, when scanning a square with a 0 on it, move right.

2. At first, when scanning a square with a 1 on it, move right.

3. The second time you meet a 0, move left.

4. The second time you meet a 1 immediately after a 0, erase the 1.

5. The next time you meet a 0 behave as if it were the first time.

6. The next time you meet a 1 behave as if it were the first time.

7. and 8. Repeat 3 and 4 then stop.

Now imagine the scanner starting at the first 0 on the left end of the tape. It moves along over the first group of 1's until it comes to the 0 between the groups of 1's and then, by 3, it moves back and rubs out the last 1 of the first group then it moves right over the next group of 1's until it reaches the last 0 on the right, it then moves back and knocks off the last 1.

After the Turing Machine operation has been finished, the tape looks as follows:

                    011111001100

The effect has been to erase two 1's from the tape. This may seem a rather pointless activity but in fact it has great significance. Suppose we use symbols q_1, q_2, q_3, ... to stand for the 'first state', 'second state', 'third state' etc., when this refers to the scanner scanning a 1 or a 0. Then $q_1 0$ means the first scan of a 0. q_2 means the next scan, although it is not *absolutely* necessary to go from q^1 to q_2 after only *one* scan in q_1. If we then add a further set of symbols such as **R**, **L**, **S** for 'move right', 'move left', 'substitute **S** for the symbol on the tape', where a special case of this last instruction is to substitute **S** where **S** = 0, this is simply the same as erasing. In the above example, substituting 0 and erasing are to be thought of as the same thing.

The symbolic version of the instructions for our above example now read as follows:

$$q_1 0 R q_2$$
$$q_2 1 R q_2$$
$$q_2 0 L q_3$$
$$q_3 1 0 q_4$$
$$q_4 0 R q_5$$
$$q_5 1 R q_5$$
$$q_5 0 L q_6$$
$$q_6 1 0 q_6$$

The instructions are made up of four symbols, two of them state symbols. The first two symbols say what the state is (e.g. first time, or next time, etc.) and what is being scanned; the second two symbols say what is to be done and whether or not you change state (e.g. if you do the same thing the next time you do not need to change state).

It should be noticed that the operation stops because when q_6 is reached and a 0 is on the tape there is nothing to do because there is no instruction starting $q_6 0$.

The reader, if interested in the technicalities of such automata methods, should consider why there was a need for repetition from q_1 to q_4 and q_4 to q_6 above. In other words, why did we not choose:

$$q_1 0 R q_2$$
$$q_2 1 R q_2$$
$$q_2 0 L q_3$$
$$q_3 1 0 q_3$$

The answer is that we could well have done so because there is no instruction starting $q_3 0$ either. Therefore, the second set is a simpler Turing Machine and does the same job as the earlier one.

If we decided to write numbers as sets of 1's, so that $111 = 3$ and $11111 = 5$, then if we also accepted the convention that the input, which is the initial state of the tape, is where all numbers are represented by one more 1 than is normal, so $11111 = 4$ and $1111111 = 6$, and the output is the normal representation with $4 = 1111$ and $6 = 111111$, we have successfully performed *addition* as in arithmetic when we erased 1 from each input number. We have put on the tape $5 + 2$ and since we read the output as the total number of 1's left, then we see that the answer is 7.

This seems an odd way of adding numbers, but the point is to show that numbers can be added in a manner which requires no intelligence, in a 'machinelike' way, in the old sense of 'machinelike'.

Turing showed that subtraction, division and multiplication, indeed *any* and *all* of the operations normally encountered in mathematics, could be performed in the same way. This meant that it was possible to write a tape with 1's and 0's and a set of instructions to process the tape in order to simulate all of the operations needed in mathematics.

The question now arises as to the way of depicting mathematics. The answer is that all mathematical operations can be depicted by recursive functions and sets taken together, where, by recursive functions, we are referring to a way of defining all of mathematics by virtue of an inductive (recursive) form of definition; it makes, if you like, mathematics into an axiomatic system.

This leads to an investigation of what is an axiomatic system in order to discover whether it has the properties of consistency and completeness, and also to discover whether it has an algorithm or decision procedure; the notion of *computability* was based on precisely this idea of an algorithm. Most of mathematics can be reproduced

algorithmically, but not all. What is left must be produced heuristically.

This brief description of Turing Machines is addressed
to a mathematical problem, but could equally well be
concerned with human thinking.

The result of much of this work has been, as we have
said, of purely mathematical importance. But one kind
of automaton is of special cybernetic interest. It is called a
neural net and will be described in some detail in the next
chapter.

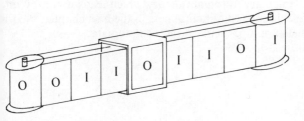

Figure 8
This is a Turing Machine, with 1's and 0's written in the squares of a
tape, which can move backwards and forwards under a scanner,
half-way between the two spools.

Summary

In this chapter we have discussed logic, starting with ordinary language, and have considered mathematical or symbolic logic. This provides general forms and rules for logical inference, regardless of the statements or classes involved.

The reason for examining logic is that logic is basic to theoretical and hardware computers and therefore to models of intelligence.

We concluded this chapter with a brief introduction to elementary automata theory which leads naturally into the discussion of neural nets in the next chapter. Neural nets are a particular kind of automata.

CHAPTER FIVE
NEURAL NETS

ARGUMENT

Neural nets should be thought of as particular types of finite automata. They are designed primarily as models of the human nervous system and, although they differ from the human nervous system in many obvious ways, they nevertheless allow us to model, and therefore to study, many of the properties of systems which are very much like human nervous systems.

They have been called both neural nets and logical nets and show the structure and function of a system which is described by a logic. Thus logical systems, such as Boolean Algebra, which we discussed in the last chapter, are also descriptions of automata. Such automata can, if necessary, be actually built from their logical description.

We have already discussed certain aspects of both hardware and software models; we have discussed logic and mathematics, which lead in turn to theoretical automata. It is known that these automata can actually be manufactured since they are based on algorithms or effective procedures. We also know that automata can be represented by digital computers, as well as by simpler models.

We now turn to automata especially designed to simulate the structure of human nerves, or neurons. Such automata are capable of being translated into tape automata, or computer programs, as needed. We shall, in this chapter, consider them simply as collections of neurons obeying certain well-defined rules.

Look at Figure 9, which shows different sorts of automata, including neural nets.

Automata, or neural nets, were first constructed in this way by Warren McCulloch and Walter Pitts (1947).

McCulloch and Pitts had in mind an artificial nervous system, which could be constructed theoretically, in this very well-defined way, from which hardware models could actually be constructed.

McCulloch and Pitts drew up neural nets as blueprints for the special senses which simulated the ability to *see*, to *hear*, to *touch*, to *taste* and so on. They also simulated the central processes of the human brain which involve the ability to learn, think and to solve problems.

We shall describe how neural nets are constructed. We shall not use the original Pitts-McCulloch notation because other simpler and more elegant notations have since emerged. The points of resemblance to the human nervous system are obvious from the way the nets are drawn up. This is so even though every user of neural nets is not necessarily interested in them as models of the nervous system, but thinks of them as systems—like automata devised for mathematical purposes—which exhibit certain logical features.

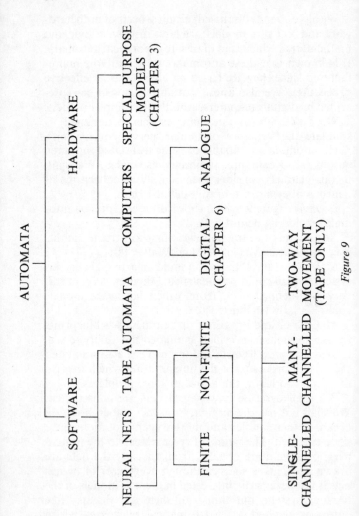

Figure 9

Figure 10 shows four neurons (or elements), represented by circles, connected in a simple net. The reason for calling them elements rather than neurons is to avoid any misunderstanding about representing actual neurons, or being called the model of actual neurons. A logical element is, in many ways, obviously different from a neuron. The circles represent the neurons or elements; on the right we draw, by tradition, the output to the neuron, while the inputs are on the left. We have several elements connected with many others. These elements can be connected in quite complicated ways but they must be connected according to well-defined rules. The rules for the connection of neural nets are relatively simple; we shall state them now.

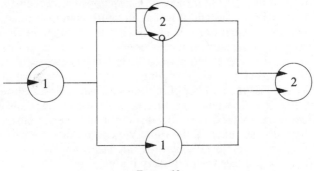

Figure 10
Four elements (neurons) connected into a simple net.

The first rule is that an output must either contain an impulse or not contain an impulse, at any instant of time. In other words, the output may ramify and go to various other elements, but these other elements will, at any instant, either receive a single pulse or no pulse at all. There is no possibility of mixing the outputs so that some outputs carry pulses and some do not; they must all be of one kind.

The second rule is that the inputs can be pulse-carrying at any instant of time and can have any pattern of 1's (which represents a pulse) and 0's (which represent the absence of a pulse) in a set of input fibres. Now these neural nets are really a geometrical rendering of Boolean Algebra. The only difference between the Pitts-McCulloch neural nets and the geometry of Boolean algebra lies in the fact that these nets have *time co-ordinates* attached to them; we have to think of this element firing at time t, and the subsequent elements at time $t+1$, $t+2$, and so on. Indeed we say that each element holds up the firing for one instant of time. The instant of time can be in any sort of unit one wishes.

All elements are supposed to take only one instant of time to fire, so that if there is one obviously non-realistic feature in the system, it is that all neurons in the human nervous system are not identical to each other in this respect. Each neuron has a *threshold*—a measure of its sensitivity—represented by the letter h, where we say that the number of excitatory inputs firing at time t must at least equal the number of inhibitory inputs firing at time t plus the constant, the threshold h. We assume, also contrary to fact, that the threshold for every neuron remains the same all the time. We can represent excitatory inputs pictorially by little filled-in triangles and we use open circles for inhibitory inputs.

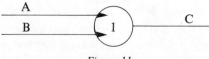

Figure 11

Let us label the inputs A and B, and the single output we will label C. The threshold of this element is 1, and we can state the condition for this element to fire as follows.

$$C_t \equiv A_{t-1} \mathbf{v} B_{t-1}$$

We say the C fires at *t*, if and only if (which is represented by the three lines ≡) *A* fires at *t* − 1 or *B* fires at *t* − 1, and where **v** means 'or' in the inclusive sense.

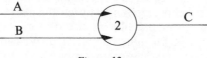

Figure 12

If we reproduce the same element with a threshold of 2, instead of 1, then our condition of firing changes so that we say that *C* fires at *t* if and only if *A* fires at *t* − 1 and *B* at *t* − 1. Both inputs must fire simultaneously to fire the neuron in the second case, whereas in the first case either of them *alone* would be sufficient to fire the neuron. The formula is

$$C_t \equiv A_{t-1} \cdot \mathbf{B}_{t-1}$$

where **.** means 'and'.

The thresholds of elements are all real numbers and they may thus include negative numbers or zero. If, however, we have a threshold of zero, an output *C* for an input *A* and need an inhibitory input, we say that *C* fires at *t* if and only if *A* does not fire at *t* − 1. In other words, the element is 'live' and fires all the time unless there is an inhibitory input; it represents the logical operator 'not'. Here is a picture and formula

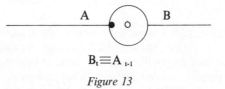

$$B_t \equiv A_{t-1}$$

Figure 13

What is so important about neural net models is that hardware systems can be built from them; they are clearly blueprints and are therefore effective. Neural nets can also, as we have seen, be represented as diagrams with elements or neurons connected by fibres, and they can be made as complicated as we need, but we can always think of them as being represented by *not* and *and* or *not* and *or*, even though in practice we use devices and elements which may be far more complicated. We can, however, always show that these more complex nets can be reduced to combinations of those which we know to be effective.

We also require one other type of element for storing information; and one obvious property of any intelligent system is that it stores information, for the storage element often used in neural nets is a loop or looped element. It seems likely here that this is neuro-physiologically realistic.

A loop element fires back on itself. The output, B for example, fires at $t+1$ if A fires at t, and continues firing indefinitely, unless, of course, there is some inhibitory input available. If such an input is not available then B will never stop. B will stop at some future time, if and only if C fires at t and A does not.

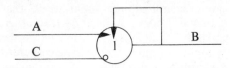

Figure 14

All elements are, as we have mentioned, the same in the neural net system; they could, of course, be made to be different, but they will all be the same in one model. All such systems are those we have called *pre-wired*. This is a matter about which some people have objected, but it does represent one of two different approaches to cybernetic problems.

Neural nets have one big disadvantage; if we have to draw 'interesting' nets, of suitable complexity, the process can become tiresome. You can represent all neural nets in the form of a matrix, and there are a number of matrix algebraic operations which represent realistic properties of the neural net representation. This algebraic representation of nets by matrices is one way to put neural nets on to a digital computer, and it is easy. There is already a language especially constructed to represent matrices on a digital computer and this is one reason why the matrix representation is useful.

We can thus handle very large collections of elements and their connection on a computer, and this is one possible approach to cybernetic modelling. Indeed a matrix representation of a neural net is simply a blueprint for an automaton.

Figures 15 and 16 show two fairly arbitrary neural nets, and the reader should try to discover their behaviour for himself.

Once we have put our logical net system on to a computer we will have taken up most of the storage space on most computers. This leads us to ask ourselves whether we can drop the well-defined structural connectivity of the neural net type of system and represent the net by something more flexible. One way to achieve this is to represent the conditional probabilities which will affect neurons. We now lose any hope of reproducing an anatomical similarity to the nervous system. On the other hand, we gain an enormous amount of space so that it may be profitable not to represent our neural nets in matrix form on a computer, but directly to program the computer to simulate what is now a more artificial and functional nervous system—an automaton which is synthesizing function, but not structure.

In the context of neural nets, we should include at least some mention of 'hardware' neural elements. Dr. Crane of the Stanford Research Institute has suggested 'Neuristor' as a name for a class of devices which purport to depict neural nets, or nervous systems, in terms of neural transmission, synaptic connections and the behaviour of individual neurons. The model suggested is in many ways an up-to-date version of Lillie's iron wire model; but it suggests ways in which nerve propogation can take place and yet still be reversible. We want to find 'fireworks' that can explode and still remain explodable.

There are many other such models, and one we should mention is due to Drs. Farley and Clark. They were able to draw up neural nets whose firing properties, when viewed on a cathode ray oscillograph, looked very similar to the graphs derived from a set of waves taken from the human brain; the evidence is gradually accumulating to make us believe that we can reconstruct much of the jig-saw puzzle of modelling the brain.

We should now state that there are many different renderings of neural nets; some of them are designed to show how, by duplicating or triplicating information in the net, we can ensure that the system is error-free. We can simulate (or at least synthesize) almost every biological system and, in doing so, many scientists have not only used the computer to represent the relevant neural nets, but have also related neural nets to information theory. Information theory is an attempt to measure the flow of information in any system. Cybernetics is, one should remember, the science of control and communication and it is easy to understand why information theory is so relevant to cybernetics.

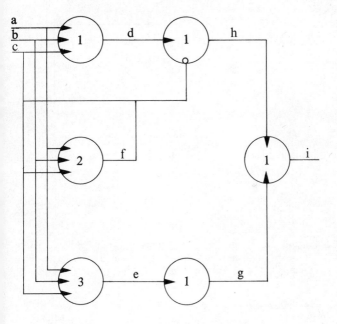

Figure 15

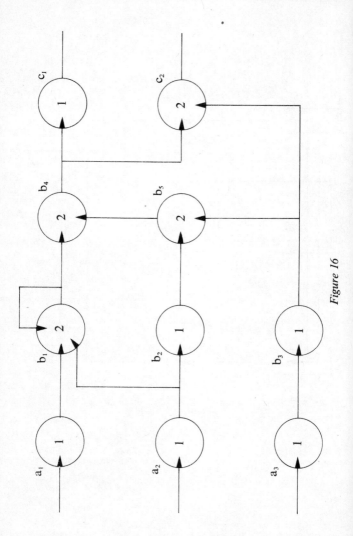

Figure 16

SUMMARY
We have in this chapter summarized neural nets in their
simplest form, showing the conventions which allow us
to draw network diagrams and write the logical formulae
which describe those diagrams. The relationship between
the drawings and the formulae is like the relationship
between geometry and algebra.

CHAPTER SIX

DIGITAL COMPUTERS AND CYBERNETICS

ARGUMENT

The digital computer is a high speed tool for performing arithmetic, indeed for performing most, if not all, of mathematics automatically and at very high speeds. The computer is a *universal* model, which is not complete until the program has been fed into it. When this is done it becomes more than a mere arithmetician, it can become an 'intelligent being' which interacts with its environment. This is the problem presented by cybernetics.

Computer programming is the most important model used by cybernetics for simulating complex systems. Computers are, when appropriately programmed, suitable models of the human being or such parts of the human being as the nervous system, the visual system, the auditory system, and so on.

Digital computers have been mentioned frequently in the first five chapters of this book, and we should now summarize some of their principal features. Digital computers are directly related to automata; they are hardware realizations of automata. Dr. A. M. Turing, who worked on the Turing Machine (an automata, which could be either finite or infinite), also played a major part in developing modern digital computers. The Turing Machine is equivalent to a digital computer if, and only if, the digital computer has access to all the punched cards or punched tape which has passed through its processor during the time that it has computed the equivalent of what is on the Turing Machine tape.

Decision procedures and algorithms, which we discussed earlier, are all relevant to the development of the digital computer since it was felt that the digital computer would perform the same role as could be performed by a decision procedure. We now know that this is not so, and that computers may be programmed to simulate human faculties other than those which are capable of being put into the form of decision procedure. The reason is that a computer can be programmed to provide *ad hoc* solutions to problems by using the same sort of rough-and-ready rules and guesses that humans use; this we call heuristic programming.

We shall now describe the organization of a digital computer.

Different Types of Computers
Computers can be classified in many different ways.

Firstly we can distinguish calculators from computers: a calculator is hand-driven and non-automatic.

An example of this class of 'computer' would be any sort of desk calculator in which there is a continual inter-action between the person using the calculator and the machine itself. The calculator is not capable of storing information, except in an extremely trivial way. It can store numbers, but not instructions, except momentarily as the cranking is in operation. Even so the calculator has played a very important part as background to the production of the modern computer.

It is of interest to note that the first calculator in com-mercial use was designed by Pascal and later modified by Liebniz.

Having distinguished the calculator from the com-puter, by saying that the calculator is manual and the computer is automatic, we now have to sub-divide the class of computers. A computer may be either *digital* or *analogue*, or even both, the so-called *hybrid*.

A digital system is one which works on a discrete number basis, so that a number is represented formally inside the system. A discrete system is one in which a digit (1, 2, 3, . . .) is either processed at any instant or is not used. To talk very generally, a piano is a discrete type of system (although not a computer). You either play or do not play a note; there are no degrees of playing. An analogue system, on the other hand, is continuous in its scale and represents its numbers by physical variables, such as currents and voltages. By analogy with the piano, the violin is an analogue type of system, which can vary its scale by degrees. The desk calculator is, in these terms, discrete in its operation but not automatic, and the slide-rule is continuous in its operation and also not auto-matic. We, as cyberneticians, are mainly concerned with digital computers. This is because of their great size, speed and accuracy. They are certainly the system which has been given the most extensive development.

Analogue computers undoubtedly will play a large and important part in the development of cybernetics and the simulation of various aspects of living organisms. Analogue computers are usually smaller than digital computers and less flexible; they play a less important part in cybernetics itself. Their most usual form is in the guise of a servo-system which performs various control operations; examples are *George* and the Watt governor, already mentioned.

We shall not, in fact, in this book discuss analogue computers further, except to say that in the opinion of many experts the human brain is partly analogue and partly digital in its operation. It is for this reason that any attempt to simulate the human brain in digital terms may seem unwise. The argument in favour of digital simulation of the human brain is that these systems can always be made to approximate to analogue ones. There is no problem involved here because, if a model is built in terms of a computer program, the actual structure will obviously be very different from that of the system simulated anyway. The question of whether the simulation of a brain, or of behaviour, can be digital or analogue may therefore seem unimportant; it is the end product that matters rather than the method; at best it is the method and not the fabric. These are, once more, the two problems of synthesis and simulation.

We shall now restrict our description of computers to automatic, electronic digital computers. The earliest digital computers were mechanical, as was the original computer design of Charles Babbage, who is, in many ways, the founder of modern digital computers. Indeed, the very first digital computers to be produced were of a design that Babbage had suggested. The only reason Babbage's own computers failed to be completed was the lack of development of precision engineering at the time his work was being done. What seemed a failure to him was in fact a major breakthrough; computers would not exist but for his work.

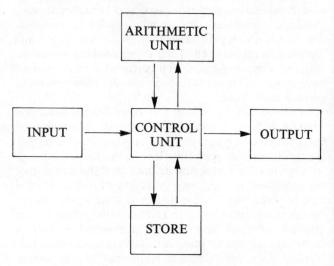

Figure 17

We can subdivide digital computers in a variety of further ways. There can be *one-address*, *two-address*, *three-address* or *n-address* computers. This distinction will be explained later. We also have computers which work in either *serial* or *parallel*. This means that they can perform their operations one at a time or many at a time; for the purpose of simulating human behaviour the latter computer is the more accurate, although even this is a matter for some debate. However, the majority of computers in commercial use are serial rather than parallel.

More important than this is the development of *multiprogramming* computers which can process many programs together. It is this feature which is more important in our comparison with the human brain.

Figure 17 is a block diagram showing the relation which exists in a computer between the control, input, output, arithmetic unit and store. Although it is true that not all modern computers have arithmetic units, the majority of them do, so that we can think of them as having arithmetic units which are completely separate from the store. The store of the computer contains both the instructions (e.g. to add, to subtract, to divide, etc.), and the numbers which are to be operated upon. The control unit then operates on the instructions, which send the numbers to the arithmetic unit for the operation to be carried out. After the operation is carried out the numbers are returned to the store. The instructions are normally in natural sequence; a computer program is the set of instructions to be sequentially obeyed, coupled with certain organizational features in the program.

Computer instructions are stated in 'words'; numbers also need to be stated in 'words' and we have in the machine *computer words* which are capable of representing both instructions and numbers; they do so normally, be it a numeric or alpha-numeric code, made up of sets of digits. So a 'word' may be something like '124678324186'. This could be either an instruction or a number.

Different computers may use different codes for their words. Many computers use *binary code* and a number of modern computers use *decimal code*. Various other codes are used, for particular purposes, as alternatives to, or in addition to, binary or decimal codes. These other codes are usually either octal (eight different digits), duo-decimal (twelve different digits), hexa-decimal (sixteen different digits), 'excess three' or binary-coded decimal. We shall say a little about these codes shortly.

It suffices to say here that ordinary English letters,

decimal numbers and all the features of everyday conversation are usually translated into a binary or some other code for the internal workings of the computer and are usually coded into the same code.

If we now assume that we have our instructions and numbers in store, the instructions start operating on the numbers. As a result the numbers are placed into the arithmetic unit, the necessary arithmetical operations are performed and the results returned to store. This is repeated again and again at enormously high speed.

To be able to phrase the instructions which are to operate on the numbers in store, we have to be capable of describing the instructions to which we are referring, and we do this by referring to the *address* of the registers in which the numbers are placed.

We can imagine, here, a simple three-address computer. A three-address computer is one whose instruction word contains three addresses: the address of the two numbers to be operated upon and the address where the result has to be placed when the arithmetical operation is completed. One-address and two-address computers operate slightly differently, usually in conjunction with what is called an accumulator. In these cases instructions simply put all numbers to be operated upon into the accumulator. These have separate instructions from the accumulator for returning them.

We can lay down, by way of illustration, the following code for our three-address computer instructions:

Add	= 01
Subtract	= 02
Multiply	= 03
Divide	= 04
Conditional Jump	= 05
Load	= 06
Print	= 07
Stop	= 08

In a real computer there will be very many more instructions than this, but here we are only concerned with illustrating the methods in simple cases. Instructions for loading information and stopping the computation are called input-output instructions, while the print and jump instructions are referred to as organizational instructions.

Let us look at a simple example. Suppose we wish to multiply 3 and 8 together and then divide by 2. We place the numbers 3 and 8 in particular registers, which we shall call 200 and 201, so that we now write 200 (3) and 201(8). We now need to use the two orders multiply (03) and divide (04). As we are using a three-address computer the structure of the instruction word is $I/A_1/A_2/A_3$, where the I (two decimal digits) tells us what operation to perform and A_1, A_2, A_3 are the three addresses. The first two addresses tell us from where to take the numbers from the store and the last address tells us where to put the numbers back into store. The three A's are addresses of the numbers to be operated upon. We can see now which instructions we need and how to write them. They are as follows:

$$03/200/201/202$$
$$04/202/203/202$$

These two instructions (which we can place in storage registers 000 and 001) are the two instructions which will multiply 3 by 8 to give us 24 and then divide 24 by 2 which is in 203 to give us 12. The computation itself is a simple one, but it shows how we write our instructions and indeed how we write a program. Programs are made up of a series of such instructions; there may be hundreds or thousands, each one performed immediately after the next, and a hundred or more being done in a fraction of a second.

Many programs of cybernetic interest may turn out to be extremely long and complicated and may be difficult

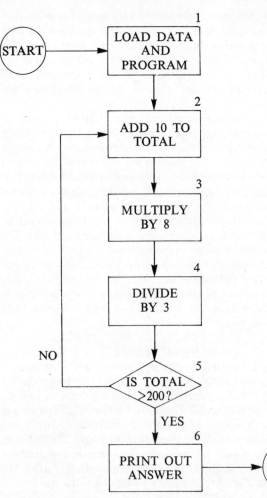

Figure 18

to 'debug'. Under these circumstances the program is often tackled in stages. First of all we clarify our ideas about how the arithmetic should be done. It must be remembered that this can be quite complicated, demanding the solution of differential equations, or some other quite complex piece of mathematics. Having decided upon the mathematical technique to be adopted, the programmer makes out his flow-chart, which shows clearly each step that needs to be taken to reach the end of the computation. Figure 18 shows a typical flow chart for a simple computation.

The programmer completes his flow chart before he writes out and codes his instructions. Eventually he punches on tape (in binary code if necessary), so that the programmed tape (set of orders) and the data tape (the set of numbers to be operated upon) are separately punched. Some machines use cards, others use tape, while some may use both, or different methods altogether; this is increasingly true as computer technology develops.

We should say next that the 'static representation' of numbers and orders is one where we consider holes punched in tape or cards. Thus a hole in a particular square of the tape or card represents a one, while the absence of a hole represents a nought. A combination of 0's and 1's represents all the digits and letters we need.

The simplicity of the binary code lies in the fact that it can be represented by any two-state switch or anything which is capable of representing only two distinguished states. The main reason the binary code was developed is the relative ease with which the hardware can cope with the representation of only two distinguished states. It should be mentioned in passing that this is one of the reasons why cybernetics pays so much attention to the development of computers—it is felt that a significant feature of the binary code used in computers is that the human brain seems to work in a somewhat similar fashion. Nerve cells either fire or do not fire—they are binary.

One of our problems in computing lies in program writing. Program writing would seem to take up so much time that the high speed of the computer, which operates at several thousand times the speed of a human mathematician, would be largely wasted because of the amount of time spent on programming. The reason this is not so is that once a program involving some complicated piece of mathematics has been written, it is stored and used again. When the same piece of mathematics comes up—even though, of course, the actual numerical data may be different—the programs may be taken from libraries and used as needed. Such stored programs are called sub-routines.

By these means a great deal of standard programming of the computer consists of the organizing of sub-routines into the main program, and switching these sub-routines out again when they have been used. It may be that we can easily specify, by editing, the steps in a lengthy and complex program by reference to portions of programs, or whole programs, already well documented and sorted in the sub-routine library.

Computer Codes
Computer codes are often in a binary form. We call the most frequently used language of computers the binary code, but we already know that the difference between a code and a language is, where it exists at all, a matter of degree. At any rate the binary code, as we have already said, depends on the use of only two primitive symbols. Since computers are concerned to a great extent with mathematical problems, it is first important to realise that our ordinary mathematical notation, the so-called decimal code with ten primitive symbols, can easily be

mapped onto a language with two primitive symbols, but not with only one. It should be made clear that by primitive symbols we mean only the actual numbers or symbols used for digits. There are, besides these symbols, other symbols for operations such as addition, subtraction, etc. The translation from binary code is simple and straightforward:

$$0 = 0000$$
$$1 = 0001$$
$$2 = 0010$$
$$3 = 0011$$
$$4 = 0100$$
$$5 = 0101$$
$$6 = 0110$$
$$7 = 0111$$
$$8 = 1000$$
$$9 = 1001 \text{ etc.}$$

For the reader who is unfamiliar with binary code, a certain amount of practice is necessary before the full simplicity of the translation is obvious.

The simplest way of regarding the matter is to realize that with only two symbols we must 'move to the left' more quickly than we do if we have ten symbols available to us. Thus, in binary counting, starting with 0 and going on to 1 we cannot go on to 2 as a separate symbol because there is no symbol which is designed to designate 2 alone. We therefore combine 0 and 1 in the same way as we do in the decimal code when we got to 10. 10 here stands for 2, and all subsequent binary numbers are combinations of the only two available symbols, 0 and 1.

In much the same way, for the decimal code, the combination of symbols 0 to 9 inclusive are the only symbols utilized after 9 has been reached. It is just a question of combining the available symbols and the fewer the symbols used the more quickly we will have to 'move to the left', because, of course, in all mathematics notation has a positional value—as 1 two places to the left in decimal code will represent 100, four places to the left will represent 10 000, six places 1 000 000 and so on. In the same way for binary code one place to the left represents 2, two places represents 4, three places 8, four places 16, five places 32, six places 64 and so on. We are, in the binary code, going up in multiples of 2 rather than multiples of 10.

This problem of translation from one language to another, of encoding and decoding, is characteristic of the machine-human relationship. The main difference here between ordinary linguistic communication and communication between the machine and the computer is that the machine and the human being are speaking different languages. The resemblance, therefore, is to a situation where an Englishman and a German or a Swiss and a Chinaman speak to each other; they have to translate word by word, or phrase by phrase, from one language to the other and vice-versa.

Where two people speaking the same language talk to each other, there is still a translation of symbols into concepts; we might ask ourselves whether there is any parallel to this in the human being 'talking' to the computer. The answer is that the operations performed by the computer could be regarded as being the equivalent of concepts represented by the language of the human being; it should be perfectly possible for the computer to have two different languages. One language is the internal binary code which is the equivalent, say, of human concepts in terms of their neural structure, and the other could be any language whatever, which refers to or describes that set of concepts; this could be ordinary English.

For purely practical reasons such a language has been found to be necessary. To explain why this is so, it should be made clear that the programming of the computer to perform either organizational or computational operations is fairly complicated, and requires a certain amount of skill and practice. It is also clear that we may expect many people to want to use the computer for some purpose and yet they have not the time, or find it worthwhile, to learn the fairly complicated programming language. So it is that they can learn a simplified language, such as a rather carefully stated version of ordinary English, which can be translated by the machine itself into the programming language.

There exist many different kinds of what we shall call autocodes. One is called an 'Interpreter' and works by using symbols which represent a computer operation, so that the whole set of computer programming operations can be represented by simple symbols. The instructions are written in the order you want them performed, or you write down the simple symbols that refer to the operations, and the machine will translate the simple symbols—they should obviously be more simple than the original ones used in the machine language or their use is pointless—one by one, by the use of a translator in the actual storage of the computer, and thus provide the necessary program.

The second type of autocode is called an 'Assembler' code and is exactly the same sort of computer language as the interpreter, except that an assembler does not depend on the translator being built into the storage of the computer in such a way that the whole operation or translation and programming occurs together. With an assembler the result of the translation is to produce a program as an output, which is subsequently fed into the computer again when it then becomes a program. The third type of computer language is called a 'Compiler' and this differs from the first two types of autocode because the number of words used in the compiler language is very much less than the number of orders that will come out in the programming language; it therefore provides a great economy of labour.

The basic idea of a compiler is that we are able to use one word to summarize a whole set of operations. For example, one may say 'find the sine of some angle', where the phrase 'find the sine of' represents or may represent a whole set of some 30 or 40 or more instructions. So the compiler code in general is very much more efficient than the assemblers and interpreters.

The fourth kind of program language is called a 'Generator'. This has so far been very little used, and is closely connected with the learning and self-modification of the machine. With a generator, the programmer needs only to specify the ends he wishes to achieve, and the computer will itself derive the necessary program by which these ends are achieved. This differs from the first three types of autocoding procedures because it makes no reference to the means whatever, only the ends. The word 'generator' has sometimes been used rather differently to refer to the application of large-scale, relatively fixed, sub-routines for specific purposes. A report program generator (R.P.G.) is an example of this type of, much simpler, generating routine.

One difficulty encountered with all these computer languages is that each computer model must have its own separate forms of autocode. But with each successive year we are gradually reaching the point where programming languages are becoming more and more interchangeable. We now have languages like FORTRAN, ALGOL, COBOL, PL1 which can be used on most computers.

One special aspect of computer languages should be mentioned; that is the attempt to produce 'nearly natural' languages, such as English, for the programming of computers. There exist a number of trial programs which vary in detail and sophistication. The first and immediate point which arises as soon as an attempt to use such a language as a compiler or generator is made is that it is necessary to eliminate vagueness. Furthermore, although private usages are acceptable, they are only acceptable provided a translation of that private usage is given at the same time as it is used. This same condition, of course, holds with any language. No objection can be held against private usage provided that the private usage is sufficiently explained. So, to use English, we should need to formalize it; that is, to make it very much more precise.

We should mention here that the present author, Dr. B. Napper at Manchester, Dr. Sarker of Rank Xerox and others have been working on languages for communication between man and computers and computers with each other. Dr. Napper's is the nearest to everyday English and is called a 'third order' compiler language.

Programs for Adaptation and Learning

It is perfectly possible for computers to learn from experience. This, indeed, underlies the idea of a generator or generating routine. If one computer operates in an environment which is unknown to it and there are some definite goals to achieve, or if one computer is playing another computer at some game, where the game is well-defined and is to be won or lost, then one computer can learn from the other; this also applies when the game is not well-defined and where the object may be to optimize some variables, i.e. to make the best use of what information it has rather than win or lose.

The simplest situation to envisage is one where one computer plays a game perfectly and the other computer playing against it does not understand the tactical rules of the game. The second computer, by imitating the tactics of the first computer, and by generalizing on those tactics, can achieve a game at least as efficient and perhaps, in certain circumstances, more efficient than the first computer. We say that it has learned from experience.

In a series of experiments in which one computer learned to play a game as a result of playing against another computer, it was clear that the computer playing the ideal game was playing from one set of rules, whereas the computer doing the learning was playing from another set. It was felt that the computer which learned to play as efficiently as the one that had started efficiently, should in fact play in exactly the same way and it is of interest to notice why it did not.

The first computer played by a set of simple rules of generalization which were translated into the computer machine language, and the second computer collected information and played by going through that collected information to see when the same sort of situations recurred. This meant that the second computer took rather longer to make decisions, as to what move was to be made in the game. It was not until generalizations about the various 'winning' situations were made that the second computer could be said to have played from certain rules. However, there could be no guarantee whatever that the same set of rules was used by the second computer as by the first; although, at best, they may represent the same tactical move, they certainly would not, in general, be represented in the same way inside the computer itself.

If we had something like a compiler code in which the first set of rules was stated, and the second computer had access to these compiler rules, could the second computer represent his rules in anything like the same way?

All of this may seem a little complicated, but it is in

fact a reminder that when learning takes place in computers which is to be anything like learning in human beings, then there must be a language available to describe what has been learned. Otherwise a computer has merely a collection of tactics used and the results, whereas what in fact it needs is a general *statement* about a whole class of similar situations. Later we shall expand on this key problem of artificial intelligence.

What has been said in this chapter applies primarily to first and second generation computers. We are now living with third generation computers and will soon be involved with fourth generation computers.

The principles involved are still the same, but the new computers are larger and faster and are able to deal with many different programs at a time. There is also an increasing development of peripheral equipment; today you can use a typewriter or video-terminal (typewriter or television or both) to program and use the computer.

The facilities which will become possible in the next decade could provide a completely new outlook on computers. It is certain that their flexibility will be increased and the increase in their overall power will be even greater.

SUMMARY

This chapter has outlined the structure of simple and typical electronic digital computers and has shown, in the broadest terms, how they can be programmed, and what their internal workings are like.

Computer languages, which are used to communicate with the computer and simplify the problem of programming, have also been discussed. These same languages are essential in the cybernetic search for artificially intelligent systems, since, without language, no system can develop humanlike intelligence.

CHAPTER SEVEN
INFORMATION THEORY AND CYBERNETICS

ARGUMENT

Information theory provides a way of measuring amounts of information passed from place to place or person to person. It is a language devised to describe the flow of information along a communication channel from a source to a destination. Information theory is a part of the theory of probability and has its origins in telecommunications; it was soon found to have a much wider range of application, and can be applied to any sort of communication, such as a conversation. It is therefore natural that cyberneticians should be interested in what is an important part of the description of a control and communication process.

We have already discussed logic and neural nets, and seen in them a means of constructing automata, especially automata similar to the structure of the human being. Information theory is closely linked to such automata but is concerned more with their function and less with their structure.

Information theory, or communication theory, as it has sometimes been called, is a mathematical expression of the general theory of communication insofar as it applies to radio, telegraphy, television or any other medium of communication whatever. The theory was originally concerned with a communication channel which was specified by a wavelength and frequency and involved vibrations of the air or electro-magnetic radiation; the process was usually continuous and represented by the mathematics of continuous function, but it could be discrete and is then described by mathematics of a different kind. Such branches of mathematics as stochastic processes are particularly relevant, since these are concerned with the mathematics of conditional probabilities.

Communication

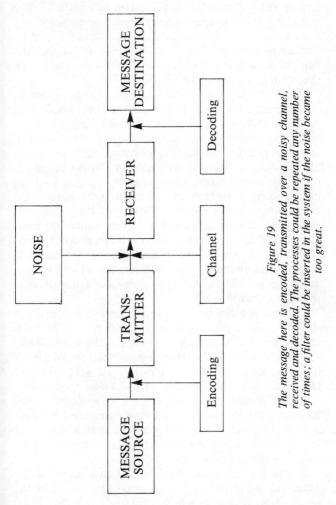

Figure 19

The message here is encoded, transmitted over a noisy channel, received and decoded. The processes could be repeated any number of times; a filter could be inserted in the system if the noise became too great.

The general communication situation in which there is a source and a destination is illustrated in Figure 18. The encoding and decoding procedure may be repeated any number of times, of course, and this involves a translation at each stage. This is much like translating from English into code, from code into Morse, and then eventually back again to English.

We have not yet mentioned a noisy channel although noisy channels do frequently occur in a communication situation. Noise is well known and can take many forms such as atmospherics in radio, or some other form of technical interference that makes it impossible to pick up all of what is being communicated. Noise occurs in everyday events, such as conversation, so that you can miss a certain amount of information by not paying attention or by being deaf. Whatever the reason, in general, information is lost when communication takes place; we shall call this loss the result of a noisy channel. To bring out the full generality of what we mean, if someone walked in front of the television while you were watching, we should say that such loss of information was due to noise.

Information can be lost when a message is sent from *A* to *B*. The clerks involved in both coding and decoding, the people actually tapping out the message and the people taking it down with paper and pencil are all liable to make mistakes. Even if there were no other factors involved, this would, in itself, make communication very much a chance matter. So we must be careful to remember that in real life communication is never completely precise. And this is independent of the problem of meaning and the extent to which we can be confused by the words we use.

One of the best known measures of information so far suggested is Shannon's. He has suggested that H be the name given to amount of information and that H be defined by the following simple formula:

$$H = -\Sigma \, p_i \log_2 p_1$$

We shall now try to show what this formula means. Σ, of course, simply means 'the sum of', so the formula is equivalent to:

$$H = - \{(p_1 \log_2 p_1) + (p_2 \log_2 p_2) + \ldots\}$$

with as many terms as you like.

The minus sign in the formula and logarithm to base 2 are conveniences for the measuring process, while the p_i's represent probabilities. They are the probabilities associated with choosing a single message from a whole set of messages to each of which a probability is associated. The minus sign allows us to have a *positive* answer, since the logarithmic term will turn out negative.

Our best proof is to see how it works in practice. Suppose there are four cards concealed from view, one of which is the ace of hearts. From our point of view they all have the same chance of being the ace of hearts since we cannot see them. Therefore since one card must be the ace the chance of any one of them being the ace will be 1/4. If we label the cards *A*, *B*, *C* and *D*, then the following table shows the odds for each:

	A	*B*	*C*	*D*
Probability of winning	3 to 1	3 to 1	3 to 1	3 to 1

Now we can say that the average amount of information passed by the system is given by our formula above. It is the sum of the logarithm of each probability multiplied by the same probability. Now we can see clearly the point of the logarithms and the minus sign. There is a theorem in the use of logarithms which says

$$\text{Log } X/Y = \text{Log } X - \text{Log } Y,$$

so, when we take the logarithm to base 2, which means log 1 is 0 (very convenient), the result is simply the positive sum of the logarithms of all the denominators. The logarithmic terms will also be minus, but the minus outside the brackets will make them plus.

$$\tfrac{1}{4} \log 4 + \tfrac{1}{4} \log 4 + \tfrac{1}{4} \log 4 + \tfrac{1}{4} \log 4$$

or, adding: $\tfrac{1}{2} + \tfrac{1}{2} + \tfrac{1}{2} + \tfrac{1}{2} = 2$

i.e., simply $\log_2 4$ which is 2. Thus we say the information is worth 2 (or since we need a name for the unit of measurement, we, in fact, say 2 bits). The word 'bit' is a contraction of the words 'binary digit' and this is explained next.

The language of arithmetic, as we might call it, is normally written, as we have already described in discussing computers, in what we call a *decimal code*. We use ten different symbols, 0 to 9 inclusive, and then repeat these symbols in combinations of the form 10, 11, 12, . . ., 20, . . ., 30, . . ., 100, . . . etc., to get as many decimal numbers as we like. The binary system makes use of two symbols 0 and 1—a language which we have seen is especially well suited to a computer—and thus we have 0000, 0001, 0010, 0011, 0100, 0101, 0110, 0111, 1000, and so on. The numbers just listed are the decimal numbers 0 to 8, written in binary form; it should be easy to see how one can go on constructing number systems using binary code, or other codes involving any number of symbols. A ternary code, for example, would be 00, 01, 02, 10, 11, 12, 20, 21, 22, 100 etc. The following table shows the conversion from decimal to binary code:

Decimal	Binary	Decimal	Binary
00	00000	12	01100
01	00001	13	01101
02	00010	14	01110
03	00011	15	01111
04	00100	16	10000
05	00101	17	10001
06	00110	18	10010
07	00111	19	10011
08	01000	20	10100
09	01001	21	10101
10	01010	22	10110
11	01011	23	10111

The translation of languages and codes is a basic part of information theory. In a sense a code is just a way of embodying ideas in a language. The word 'code' used above is quite appropriate because it certainly is a system of symbols for representing numbers; for that matter any words in English can be produced in binary code. In Morse we can encode ordinary English sentences, and here we use a ternary code involving dot, dash and pause. If we used just a dot (or dash) and a pause we should have a binary code. A language can be said to be an interpretation of the code.

The point of having 2 bits (or binary digits) as our measure of information in the above example of card drawing was that, if we send a message saying that any one of the cards had been picked (not knowing in advance which card it would be), you would need four distinguishable messages to represent A, B, C and D. This requires just 2 binary digits, i.e., 00, 01, 10 and 11 therefore we say the average flow of information in the channel will be 2 bits. 3 bits would be used to represent a game with 8 cards, and so on. This illustrates our method of measuring information flow. We can thus be seen to be able to measure information, or at least the average rate of information flow, from a particular source. Similarly we can say that when a message is passed we can give a measure of what information that message contains. If A is the card, the message contains $\log_2 4$, or 2 bits. If the probabilities had not all been the same in our card example, we should see that the average amount of information would not necessarily be the same as the information given by a single message, which is simply $\log_2 p_i$, where the particular p_i implied is the probability of that particular card being drawn. Therefore, if the cards were given probabilities 1/8, 1/8, 1/4 and 1/2 for A, B, C and D respectively, then the message telling us D was the card would be worth 1 bit.

In other words our measure of information takes account of what we regard as unlikely; if we are told something unexpected, we should receive more information than if we were told something expected. The limiting case in this matter of information is when we are told something we know, or which is certain, and then the message has no bits of information at all.

Quite clearly the greater the odds against an event, the more information given if you tell us it has happened or correctly tell us it will happen, assuming we do not already know. Similarly the maximum possible information for the system as a whole must occur with the maximum uncertainty, and this is when the probabilities are equal.

The channel capacity of a system is clearly related to our problem. A measure for channel capacity, in the simplest case where all the probabilities are equal, is fairly easy to arrive at. If we have an alphabet A, B, ... etc. of 16 symbols—these symbols could be the names of cards or they could be letters in an alphabet—and if each symbol is of the same duration, thus carrying 4 bits of information each, then the capacity of the channel is $4n$ bits per second, where the channel is capable of transmitting n symbols per second. A more complicated measure applies when the symbols are all of the same duration and where the probabilities are unequal. We are not, however, concerned so much with the details as with illustrating the method.

The duration of the symbol deserves some further mention. If we are transmitting any message whatever in code, we need punctuation. If we do not have some form of punctuation then symbols become confused with each other, like letters running together. It is perhaps easiest to think of the Morse code here. If we sent three successive dots and could not use a pause, which is really a sort of punctuation mark, then we would not know whether there were three E's, an I and an E or an E and an I or a single S: the pause acts as a punctuation mark. Similarly if all the words in an English message were run together, it might be difficult to disentangle individual words.

As with many operations, the order is important. You cannot pick up a telephone which is already picked up; you cannot go through a door-space without first opening the door. The order is a vital factor, and the description must be ordered and unscrambled. Punctuation deals with order in language, and one other possible solution, often used in computers—which generally use binary code—is to have a fixed word-length. So, every 32 binary symbols, say, make up a word. If your word happens to be simply '10' (just the two symbols) then it is still preceded by 30 0's and reads

00000000000000000000000000000010.

The mathematical theory of information now goes on to develop theorems about information flow, showing the minimum size of channel necessary to communicate certain messages at a certain rate, and the most economical way of coding messages to maximise speed or accuracy or some other such variable in the transmission of messages from a source to a destination.

Information Theory and Natural Language
In natural language we have a system of symbols, in the form of words and pauses, which allows information content to be measured; hence it is susceptible to the treatment of Information Theory. This also presents difficulties. If we wish to use Shannon's measure of information, we have to consider the totality of possible words or sentences which *might* be used to assess the probability that any particular set should be used. However, although this seems difficult, it is in fact clear that, with language, a certain choice is involved; the use of one word in a sentence, or the use of a sentence in a paragraph, limits the choice of further words or sentences. They are constrained by both the subject matter and the structure of English sentences.

An example of these constraints operating on the choice involved in language is simple; it is only necessary to consider the present sentence. Having started with 'An' I would be unlikely to follow it with 'An', but likely to follow it with a noun; having said 'An example' it is almost certain that I shall use a preposition. It is easy to see that with each successive word the rest of a sentence becomes increasingly constrained until many sentences will have no choice left when the last word is reached.

It is the continuity in discussion which allows the loss of information without total loss of sense. The property of so-called statistical homogeneity is a vital one here. We know that a series of sentences are likely to have a definite relation to each other, and that a book dealing with animals or football is likely to keep to the subject, and this allows us a limited domain from which we have to guess the missing details of words or even whole sentences. These properties of redundancy and homogeneity are what allow us to 'break codes'.

The idea that any one symbol could destroy the whole meaning of the actual message is clearly not a practical possibility since no language ever includes such wholesale coding, and every symbol must have some relation to the next . . . this is what is meant by the context of a discussion if it is to be a sensible one.

Redundancy is a special concept, which can be given a precise measure. If we say that the *relative entropy* of a system is the degree of actual information passed as a percentage of the amount of information that *could* have been passed, the complement of this is called the redundancy. In other words, the smaller the relative entropy, the larger the redundancy. In practice basic English has great redundancy. Since the vocabulary is small, things take a great deal of saying, so this lengthens any statement or description and does so with considerable redundancy. On the other hand 'Finnegan's Wake' or 'Ulysses', the celebrated novels of James Joyce, have little redundancy because they use new words in place of whole phrases in basic English; they cut down the length of the description at the expense of greatly enlarging the vocabulary, and so make glossaries of terms necessary.

Information Theory and Stochastic Processes

Conditional probabilities, which we have seen as being so useful to describing intelligent activity, lead to a method of description called 'stochastic processes'. A stochastic process is really a random series, a series of symbols (let us use A, B, C, . . .) which occur in a purely random way, and for which a definite probability can be associated with the occurrence of each symbol. Thus for the following table:

A	$\frac{1}{8}$
B	$\frac{1}{4}$
C	$\frac{5}{8}$

Table 1

a series such as:

> *BBACCACCC*
> *BCCCCCB*

might be regarded as typical. The longer the series, the more likely it is to conform to the table, unless the table is derived from the series. The process can be carried out in either direction. One direction, that of compiling the table, is *learning*, and the other, that of defining the series from the table, is what is sometimes called *performance* and is based on learning.

If the series leads to the table we often refer to the fractions in it as 'conditional probabilities', and we say that the fraction, or probability, associated with each letter of the alphabet, gives the ratio of occurrence of that letter to the total number of letters occurring.

We can now consider two successive events, so that we may have a table of conditional probabilities extending over two such events. As an example, using the same alphabet of A, B and C alone, consider:

	A	B	C
A	1/4	3/4	0
B	7/10	1/10	1/5
C	1/4	1/2	1/4

Table 2

which may generate a series such as:

CABABCBABABABAAABABAA
BCCBABABB

Note that A can *never* be followed by C.

We can have a conditional probability table over three successive events, e.g.:

	AA	AB	AC	BA	BB	BC	CA	CB	CC
A	0	0	1/3	0	0	1/6	1/3	0	1/6
B	0	0	2/5	0	0	1/5	2/5	0	0
C	1/10	3/10	1/10	1/10	0	1/5	1/10	0	1/10

Table 3

Again we can generate series with the conditional frequencies of the letters A, B and C, as depicted in Table 3.

The particular stochastic process which deals with successive probabilities is referred to as a Markov Chain. With such Markov Chains we can reconstruct English or any other language so that, if we consider conditional probabilities over as many as seven consecutive letters of the English language, including one letter for a space between words, then a fair approximation to English can be achieved. One may guess that in the table for English will be found the column headed U, in the row for Q, for two successive letters, being very nearly 1, since Q is nearly always followed by U in English. We could, of course, also reconstruct English in terms of words, and not letters.

In sensible English we always find the property of statistical homogeneity. This property of statistical homogeneity can be used in a special way, and for many purposes. Different authors tend to build up slightly different vocabularies, and as a result it is possible to carry out statistical tests to establish the authors of anonymous works by noting the frequency with which certain words occur. Such a test of vocabulary tends to be as critical for each author as a test of fingerprints.

It is possible at this point to see the significance of the Markov Chain because the discussion of conditioning and signs and the behaviouristic theory of language, which came earlier, was a theory about events following each other in a specified order. A Markov Chain is a way of specifying that order. An ordering of symbols which tends to repeat itself with some regularity is called 'ergodic'. In fact an ergodic source is one that has precisely this property of being statistically homogeneous. The world seems to be ergodic; if it were not we could have no science and no prediction.

Finally, we should say that there exist many models of learning and perception, equivalent to our hardware models of chapter three, and they will be discussed further in the next two chapters. These discussions should clarify the relationship between brain function, human behaviour and our various methods of measuring and modelling.

Before leaving this chapter we should mention Ashby's law of Requisite Variety. This says in effect that in a two-person game the variety possible is determined by the number of possible choices open to the two players. If **B** alone has a choice and his opponent **A** has none (this is what is called a 'Game against Nature'), then the variety involved is that of **B**'s choices alone. If we give **A** some choices then the variety of choices begins to diminish so that we can reduce variety as a function of the number of choices.

To the statistician, this argument is reminiscent of that about degrees of freedom; to common sense, it is saying 'If your opponent widens his choice of retaliations, then he reduces your choice of actions'. Information processing and Theory of Games are both reminders of limits that can be placed on information processing.

Summary

Information theory is a language or code for describing communication systems. The use of information theory, which is a part of probability theory, enables us to measure the amount, the flow and the channel capacity of any communication system. Information can apply to telecommunications, to ordinary conversation or to the way we see and hear things. Communication is a central theme of cybernetics.

We have, in this chapter, described Shannon's measure of information flow, and discussed other concepts such as redundancy and channel capacity.

Most important of all, from the cybernetic point of view, we have related the notions about information to the methods called stochastic processes—these are a part of probability theory—and relate to learning, adaptation and language. They also suggest a relevant process to incorporate in an automaton.

Finally, we mentioned the law of requisite variety which directly bears on control and decision taking, especially in the context of games (strategies) played by many different people.

CHAPTER EIGHT

HUMAN BEHAVIOUR AND CYBERNETICS

ARGUMENT

Cybernetics is concerned with psychology because psychology is concerned with the behavioural patterns of organisms which adapt to changing circumstances.

The development of psychological theories of cognition, particularly with respect to learning and perception, mirrors closely the attempt by cyberneticians to model these same adaptive processes in what we have called 'machines'.

Basic Concepts

We now discuss psychology—the science of behaviour—and its relation to cybernetics. In one sense we could categorize psychology as the common ground of cybernetics and biology. However, this is vague and will not be sufficient to make clear the relations that actually exist between the various parts of the biological and social sciences. Psychology overlaps cybernetics, for the most part, in the field of cognition—the science of learning—perception and thinking.

Psychology as a complete science is not to be identified with psychiatry or abnormal psychology. The primary problem of the science of behaviour is to give predictive accounts of what we call 'normal behaviour'. Added to this is the, admittedly very important, problem of accounting for abnormal variations.

Psychology, as a science, is in much the same situation as any other science because behaviour, unlike physics, chemistry or biology, can be investigated at many different levels of precision. We can ask why Mr. Smith behaves the way he does, and we can explain his motives in terms of his observed behaviour. We can also explain his behaviour in terms of his motives, as far as we understand them.

We can also investigate the underlying physiological changes accompanying the observable behavioural changes. Indeed, these very physiological changes can also be investigated at the level of chemical and physical change. It is not that each level of explanation is necessarily complete in itself, but that each offers a different aspect of the behaviour of the organism as a whole. It is impossible to make any distinctions between these different levels and the different forms of explanation they entail. In particular, it makes little sense to try to draw any serious distinction between physiology and psychology. However, we may broadly say that psychology is concerned with the organism's behaviour, as a whole, when couched in terms of what we can observe publicly. It is rather like analyzing a golf ball in terms of how it is used, on the one hand, and how it is constructed on the other. The first is psychology; the second physiology.

If we concentrate on pure psychology (as opposed to its applications) we shall have two main problems very broad in their scope; they have been called the 'theory of perception' and 'theory of learning', and they are two main features, but not the only ones, in discovering how people think.

Let us say that perception is concerned with the way human beings gather information about the outside world; the way they sense, or, in particular, the way they see, hear, feel, etc. Perception is the process of interpreting sensory, or incoming, signals. Learning is concerned with adaptation and is not wholly separable from perception. It is concerned, of course, with how organisms are able to modify themselves according to their experience.

Learning, in its simplest form, can be illustrated by an experiment carried out by Yerkes. He trained an earthworm to run along a T-shaped maze, which had dried leaves at one end of the short arms of the cross-piece of the T, and had an electrified grille in the other arm. The worm received a shock when he turned to the right and found dried leaves (apparently desirable to earthworms) if he turned left. These directions can, of course, be interchanged without affecting the experiment providing they are not interchanged during the experiment. After some hundreds of trials the earthworm always learned to turn away from the shock and toward the leaves. This is one of the simplest examples of what the psychologist means by learning, and it is an exact equivalent of the cybernetic maze runner. The fact is that some modification has been introduced into the earthworm which changes his behaviour. That there are also neural changes taking place is fairly clear when one sees that the earthworm still retains his skill after his primitive brain—two small ganglia at the head end—is removed but when the nervous tissue regenerates and grows new ganglia the skill is lost. This example is not only of interest in demonstrating what we intend by 'learning'; it also suggests the sort of role the nervous system might—in a very general way—be expected to play in learning.

One of the most obvious differences between cybernetic maze-runners and the earthworm is that the earthworm takes several hundred trials to acquire the necessary learning, while the cybernetic maze runner requires only a very few. It can, in fact, deal with a simple T-shaped maze in one trial.

Let us next remind ourselves of variations between two different individuals. If we have two men who, in the past, have behaved in different ways in the same circumstances, we shall not be surprised if they behave in different ways in the future. Mr. Brown has always been sensible and Mr. Smith stupid. The very fact of classifying them as 'sensible' and 'stupid' springs from observations, descriptions and interpretations, sometimes true and sometimes false, made by other people. When there is the need to perform some sensible act in the community and Mr. Brown and Mr. Smith are both faced with this situation, then we shall predict that Mr. Brown will succeed and Mr. Smith will fail. Most predictions are more complicated than this, since most people are not easily classified as sensible or stupid. They are usually something of a mixture of the two, and circumstances are not usually repeated in exactly the same way.

Theories of Behaviour

Psychology, in its earliest days, was based mainly on introspections. The idea was that there was something

called a 'mind' which operated, and somehow controlled
the body. It is true that some people still talk in these
terms, which is harmless provided that in the word
'mind' we are merely using a shorthand for the controlling aspects of behaviour, without implying that there is
a mind that is separable from a body. Perhaps a better
analogy is between a car and its performance, for body
and mind are as much one as a car and its engine. The
idea of body and mind being separate entered psychology
at its beginning and, for a very long time, had a considerable influence. For somewhat the same reasons that the
notion of a separate 'mind' has been kept alive, there has
also been kept alive a *vitalistic* view of behaviour, which
conceives of behaviour in terms which cannot be described or performed in a purely mechanistic way.
Holders of vitalistic views are responsible for great
emphasis being placed on 'instincts' and 'insights',
because these seem to provide a block to mechanistic
progress. A great deal of work on higher apes produced
evidence to show that their intelligence was dependent on
insight, and this was thought to be non-machine like,
and therefore incapable of being reproduced by any sort
of machine.

A famous example is that of Kohler's ape 'Sultan'
who was able to solve the problem of reaching a banana
which was further away than either of his two sticks
could reach. He fitted the two sticks together so that he
then had one stick long enough. He was not shown how
to do this, and it seemed to depend on his being able to
see the situation as a whole. The Gestalt school of psychology has made the most of such evidence in insisting on
the importance of perception in learning, a fact that is
now widely accepted. One of the points cyberneticians
have made again and again is that insight is not a barrier
to a machine equivalence, but merely means that we
have to broaden our ideas about machine-like processes.

To put it another way, we are reminding the reader of the ambiguity of the word 'machine'. We really mean 'something which is capable of being made *artificially*'. In fact, in the higher examples, it is not machine-like but an organism.

The most famous experiments on learning theory, which had a cybernetic ring about them, were those of Pavlov. These are called experiments in conditioning, and the behaviour illustrated is called 'conditional reflex' behaviour. The experiments can best be described by taking a simple example. Imagine a dog harnessed in a sound-proof room and subjected to the following stimulation. Some food is presented to him, at the sight of which he salivates. Then, after a while, a bell is rung whenever the food is presented. Then, after many trials, in which the bell and the food are presented together, the ringing of the bell alone is sufficient to elicit saliva-tion. Clearly the dog would not salivate, before the experiment started, to the sound of the bell alone, so we say that he has been *conditioned* to salivate to the sound of the bell. It is as if the bell were a *sign* to him that food was about to be presented. This represents the basic notion of conditioning.

From these simple beginnings much more complicated associations can be built up. The assumption of the early behaviourists was that all behaviour was essentially of the same form as that described, and that all seemingly complicated activity consisted of more or less compli-cated forms of conditioning. This is still the belief of some behaviourists, although many would now take a some-what broader view of a 'reflex' than that implied by Pavlov's early experiment. Part of the evolution of learn-ing theory, and, indeed, of science in general, has been to change terminology from time to time. It is not so much that the ideas or concepts the words stand for are neces-sarily different, but that certain words get overworked;

they get emotional overtones attached to them and then they are dropped for a while. Sometimes, as in the case of the word 'instinct', such terms return to fashion when the original battle has died down. This is also the case with conditional response or conditional reflex terminology. Most of modern learning theory has dealt with the same development in different terms.

Automata and Behaviour

We can now use the neural nets developed in chapter 5 to show how conditioning may operate. In the following net we are using the elements to represent not single neurons, but whole collections, and the emphasis should not here be placed on the notion of neurons at all. We are simply saying that an automata built this way would show a Pavlovian type of conditioning.

Let us suppose we have a black box (we can imagine this to be an organism) which we cannot open. We have to guess what changes happen inside whenever there is a change in external conditions. It is now necessary to construct the sort of mechanisms which are supposed to operate inside the box. This is a sort of imaginary physiology which is sufficient to give a consistent account of the external behaviour of the black box. The neural net goes beyond being a black box and suggests a possible mechanism in a way which is fairly close to 'real' physiology.

More General Conditioning

We can now generalize the classical conditioning experiments by extending the terms of conditioned-response theory to more general kinds of behaviour. There is what is called type II, or instrumental conditioning, incorporating four types of training: reward training, escape training, avoidance training, and secondary reward (or symbol) training. We shall give brief examples of these four types of behaviour.

123

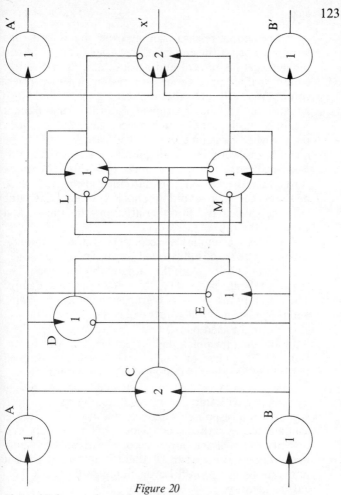

Figure 20
*If A and B fire together, C fires and then M (which stays 'live') and this reduces the threshold of x' to **1**, so that if A or B fire alone thereafter x' fires. But if this happens, either D or E is fired—which extinguishes M and starts L; now x' has a threshold of **3**, so that even A and B firing together will not fire x'. All sorts of patterns of association can be built on such a net.*

In one simple reward-training experiment a rat runs a maze to be, at the end of it, rewarded. The rat has to move to get his reward and he does not, as in classical conditional, require to be strapped in a sound-proof room. We will describe the escape and avoidance situation in a single experiment. If a rat is running in a rotating wheel, part of which is electrified, and we shock the rat when he is on the electrified part, he will escape from the situation by running until he is away from this electrified part. If we now sound a bell before the shock starts, then the rat will be conditioned to run as soon as he hears the bell, to avoid the shock. It is much the same as in the classical conditioning situation; the bells act as a *signal* to the rat.

Our next example is secondary reward training. Secondary reward is illustrated by apes who are trained to perform simple tasks if they are suitably rewarded. The rewards take the form of red, blue and brass poker chips. The red chips are worth two grapes, the blue, one grape, and the brass, none. The apes will work, pick out the red chips from a mixed pile as their reward, and when these have all gone, they pick the blue and leave the brass untouched. They have, of course, initially to be conditioned to the relative values of the chips. We now outline, briefly, a general theory of learning as it might appear today. The theory will start, as in conditioning theory, with stimulus and response as undefined notions. The idea is that a stimulus activates behaviour; the set of responses it elicits is the behaviour observed. The organism usually needs to be motivated to be able to respond at all, but motivations are plentiful even though sometimes difficult to identify.

The basic motivations are probably survival, food, sex etc.; all the means that are associated with these basic motivations become secondary motivators. If motivated, then, the organism will respond to the stimulation. The nature of his response will depend on his previous experience of this, or what are perceived of as similar situations. There will be a general tendency to retain memories or habits which contribute toward a state of affairs satisfying to the organism—the state of *homeostasis* illustrated in part by Ashby's Homeostat (Chapter 3)—and not to reproduce habits which are not satisfying to the organism.

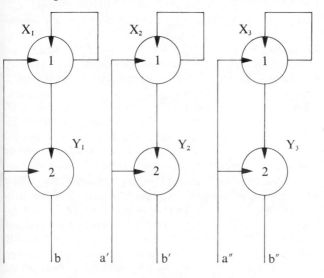

Figure 21
When any combination of a, a' and a'' fire so does the equivalent
x, and it stays 'live' reducing the threshold of its equivalent y by 1;
if an a-pattern fires again, the equivalent output at b tells us which
of the x's are 'live' and which are not.

Any intelligent interaction between an organism and its environment depends upon a memory store which allows it to classify experiences (Uttley's and Chapman's models), so that some process of comparison can take place between the present situation and situations that have occurred in the past. The cat that has narrowly escaped with his life in his meeting with a dog, say, will have learned that any situation in which a dog is present is dangerous, particularly if it involves the same dog which frightened him before, and to a similar, if decreasing, extent for all other dogs. Of course, some of these responses may be instinctive, innate or learned very early in life. The ability to distinguish different situations, whether by touch, smell, vision or hearing, is a matter involving us in perception, so we shall consider that next. But before we do so, let us show another neural net of a memory store and remind the reader of the similarity of our very general theory to the structure of computers.

Perception and Automata

Perception and learning are almost wholly intertangled. Perception is not the same as merely sensing (seeing or hearing) since it involves interpretation of what is seen or heard. Furthermore it is difficult to study because we cannot assume that, because there is actually some object in the field of view of an organism, he will necessarily perceive it. He may or he may not, and whether or not he does so depends upon attention, and, perhaps, his motivation at the time. It is there *to be* perceived; we can perceive it and many others may also perceive it, so that it is almost certainly not an illusion, but still the fact remains that any one person may not perceive it. If he fails to perceive a sign in the way we expect, then his behaviour will generally be different from what we have expected.

In the computer, our sensing processes are simulated by the reading of punched tape or cards and the perceptual processes contribute all the environmental factors to the input information, as well as that contained in previous experience. All he knows, other than anything he may have innately acquired, is learned through perception and therefore by use of the special senses. To use vision as our example, the process can be likened to that of a camera which takes snapshots and leaves the brain to interpret them. This is a reminder that, if the inputs to a computer are like seeing itself, perception is a combination of inputs with the memory store (the interpreting). It is obvious that inputs form an essential part of learning. And, if there is no memory of previous experience, no interpretation is possible since interpretation means precisely the process of classification in the light of what has happened to the organism previously.

Cyberneticians are concerned, of course, with the modelling of perceptual processes, and many different models are in existence. There have also been many disagreements as to which of the various models—all of which can be shown to be workable to a greater or lesser extent—is most similar to the human visual system. Perception is a subject, of course, which should be regarded from the point of view of all the senses taken together. Therefore arguments about perception sound over-simple when vision is considered alone. Ultimately, all the senses work together, and the process of perception is not wholly distinguished from that of conceptualization. But pattern recognition is the process involved at all stages; some form of classification seems to be the appropriate method of achieving it.

What has been said, all too briefly, may be summarized as follows. Learning and perception operate together and, with the associated factors of thinking, imagining, motivation and the like, are the subjects of controlled experiment and observation designed to help us to understand human behaviour. It is certainly possible that the process of learning should be distinguished from that of merely retaining information, simply because the human being is more active in his selection of his possible behaviour patterns. It is, perhaps, self-evident that the more we learn about physiology, biochemistry, biophysics, and genetics, the more we can fill in the gaps in our knowledge of the organism. Furthermore, it is fairly clear, in principle, how the pieces of the jigsaw fit together.

The totality of facts about organisms is tremendously complicated. But viewed from every point of view, these presently scattered facts will one day be the basis of what we shall no doubt think of as 'human biology', and very much *a part of* cybernetics.

Behaviour and Cybernetics

We must now deal more explicitly with the link between psychology and our main theme of cybernetics. The overlap is quite clear, since both subjects are concerned with communication and control. It should be said, though, that there is no complete agreement about the relation of cybernetics to psychology. But we can propose the matter this way: cybernetics tells us that all control and classification systems, all communication systems, have certain common characteristics, which allow us to describe them in terms of their feedback and control mechanisms. This description fits in with the more recent behaviourist movement; cybernetics is prescribing a form of approach which allows us to state our theories of behaviour in a roughly-known pattern of great generality.

Cybernetics, of course, encourages the use of the mathematical methods already employed in control engineering, in such fields as statistical thermodynamics and other related disciplines from engineering to physics.

We can see from this that a human being can be regarded as a machine, with a kind of classification system working in a particular way—and its working emphasizes the importance of the problem of perception. Beyond the classification of the sensory inputs, we have the control systems with their feedback loops and storage which emphasize the problem of learning. We should go on from this to consider both synthesis and simulation of problem-solving, thinking and decision-taking; at that point we are dealing with the complete problem of human intelligence.

A cybernetic model of behaviour can be provided by a computer simulation, by building neural nets or other automata—whether in software or hardware. In each case the object must be to show part or all of human cognitive behaviour. Inputs are associated with sensing (seeing, hearing, etc.) and this involves, when perception occurs, the memory store. Many models have been suggested, and the reader should certainly remember the classification models. Simple learning was achieved by the Grey Walter 'tortoise' and the maze-runners. Ashby showed something of purposiveness or goal-seeking with the Homeostat, and as we graduate to more complex cognitive processes so we need increasingly to think of computer simulation. Cyberneticians believe that behaviour generally is a sort of deductive-inductive procedure and one for which a machine, however complex, can be an adequate model. This means the machine must be capable of logical inference and of using a language.

Learning, Language and Automata

We already have a clear picture of simple learning which is, in essence, the selective reinforcement of certain associations and processes. The results of learning are necessarily stored inside the computer otherwise they cannot be manifested in performance. The methods used for simple adaptation, and learning, are not, however, appropriate to more complex problem-solving at the level of human behaviour. The well-known and obvious reason for this is that the forming of a simple algorithm or decision procedure is not always possible. There is also more complicated behaviour, increasingly dependent on the human ability to symbolize a problem: to describe it in either mathematics or ordinary language. This leads us to the field of **heuristics**.

We shall think of heuristics as being similar to beliefs or hypotheses which are, usually, arrived at inductively, and which need to be confirmed or disproved by experience. This is the method of arriving at solutions to problems, where neither the problem nor its solution is clearcut. We are imitating now the human being who is told to change the organization of his factory to improve the through-put. He says 'move all of contract 360 to factory B and cancel all contracts between 40 and 50', and so on. Figure 22 shows a simplified flow chart of the sort of processes envisaged.

This is the beginning of a process that typifies all of human activity.

We shall say no more about it here, but return to these matters again, especially in Chapter Ten, when we talk about Management Cybernetics.

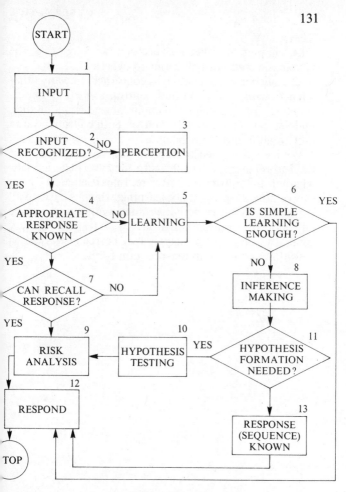

Figure 22

*This schematic flow chart shows stages, in the analysis of an
input, characteristic of the heuristic process. The final stage of risk
analysis (9) considers what the cost will be (risk entailed) if you
are wrong.*

SUMMARY
This chapter has been concerned with relating the systematic study of behaviour to cybernetics.

The science of psychology is concerned, like any other science, with prediction and control, as well as understanding. In this field the main object is to predict, understand and ultimately control, both collectively and individually, human behaviour.

We have discussed perception and learning and have tried to relate these problems to the cybernetic models, whether in hardware or software. In particular, we have shown how the property of learning, which is basic to all the higher cognitive activities, such as thinking, can be reproduced in automata. In fact we have shown, very generally, how the principles can be reconstructed in neural net or in computer program form.

CHAPTER NINE
BIOCYBERNETICS

ARGUMENT

Physiology, especially neurophysiology, is concerned with the internal biological organisation of the human being. It is concerned with the construction of models made of nerve cells and these are the cells which we shall think of as basic building-bricks for our own models.

Homeostasis is the principle of adjustment to external conditions in order to retain a state of stability inside the organism. This principle supplies one direct link between cybernetics and physiology in general, and with neurophysiology in particular. The other link is that of the idealized nerve cells of neural nets and the closeness with which they can be made to approximate to natural nerve cells.

Cybernetics and Biocybernetics

Biocybernetics is a branch of cybernetics; it is that branch which is concerned with the modelling of biological systems. Physiology and anatomy deal with the function and structure of the body. Human neurophysiology and human neuro-anatomy deal with the function and structure of the human nervous system, and this is of cybernetic interest, since it is concerned with the function and structure of the best known of all feedback systems, the human being. We shall concentrate mainly on the human nervous system, for it is at this point that the problems of behaviour and cybernetics come closest together.

Many behavioural problems are clearly capable, in principle, of description in neurological terms. That is, we may observe and describe a simple response, such as a knee-jerk, by reference to the nerves which travel to and from the knee. We must go further than this and say that it is desirable to reformulate our description in a biological language, for which the observed behaviour has already been directly described.

The problem is that of opening the black box and observing the mechanisms. That it is not possible to put this program fully into practice at the moment is due to the enormous complexity of the mechanisms and the inconvenience involved in opening the black box. It is not necessary that we should think in neurological terms in analyzing behaviour, but it is desirable from the point of view of integrating our scientific knowledge, because we do not seem to be able to achieve the necessary degree of predictability by psychological theories which are not aided by biological detail.

Behavioural problems must first be described in behavioural terms, then in neurological terms, and then, very much later, it may be possible to redescribe them in biochemical and biophysical terms. The whole of this plan must in any case depend upon the development of the rest of the biological sciences. Indeed, the present knowledge of the biochemical and biophysical aspects of the nervous system does not accord much immediate hope for very rapid development, at least for the second stage of the plan. Such a program is sometimes called 'reductionist'. The problem of describing behaviour in neural terms is very considerable and the problem of testing such hypotheses as may be forthcoming may be even more difficult. But this research is actually now in progress, and before we consider some of the possibilities, it may be useful to reflect on those aspects of neurology and neurophysiology which are relatively well-established.

The central nervous system (the peripheral nervous system, while important, is less relevant to the control of behaviour) has often been compared to a complex telephone system, where the higher centres and synapses, which are the connecting points of nervous tissue, are seen as similar to telephone exchanges. This analogy is useful up to a point and a fairly natural one to adopt in what is obviously a *communication* network.

All nerve fibres are elongations of the nerve cells, and they ramify throughout the entire body. The cells situated in the grey matter of the spinal tracts, and the brain itself (central nervous system), have a common origin with the other nerve cells (peripheral nervous system) and other body cells which make up the whole organism.

During evolution, nerve cells have become specialized in their role of communication links. This, of course, is not to say that the property of information transmission is wholly excluded from other types of cell tissue. However, it is certainly far less marked in these other cells because of the presence of special nervous tissue; this removes from the other tissue the main burden of information transmission. Nerve cells have a cell body and many short-range off-shoots, called dendrites, and usually a single long-range off-shoot called an axon. Nerve cells can be categorized according to the number of such off-shoots each nerve body has.

The brain itself is made up of tracts, connecting layers of grey cells, and is a modified, highly specialized, head-end of the spinal cord. The form of specialization taken is seen most clearly in comparative terms. If an inspection is made of the nervous system of the earth-worm, the frog, the rabbit and so on, in steps of increasing complexity, we can see the form evolution has taken over very long periods of time. The simplest invertebrates, such as amoeba, have no specialized nerve cells. In the earth-worm the two principal nervous strands running throughout its length can be clearly seen, with two, more or less specialized, nervous knots, or ganglia (collection of neurons), in the head-end. The leading end is, of course, also the end of maximum sensitivity: it is the beginnings of a simple brain.

Man's central nervous system is made up of about 10^{10} or 10^{11} neurons, according to an estimate of Professor Warren McCulloch, the American neurologist. The complexities involved in possible combinations of such a number defy imagination. We do not know for certain how the connections actually correlate with the processing of the information.

The human brain is conveniently, if rather arbitrarily, divided into sections—largely as a result of embryo-logical evolution—and from the top of the spinal cord, going up through the brain, we have first the *medulla oblongata*, then the *midbrain*, and then the *pons varoli*. The *medulla* is probably a reflex mediating centre (tele-phone exchange) containing certain nuclei, or aggrega-tions of nerve cells, and the same is probably true of both the *midbrain* and the *pons*; the details, plotting of tracts, etc. are of considerable complexity. The *cerebellum*, a large motor organ attached behind the principle mass of the brain, is concerned with equilibrium and posture.

The *thalamus* and *hypothalamus*, which are genetically old, are concerned with the reflex mediation of 'emotional' responses. It was probably once the controlling part of the brain; now it has become an end-station on the sensory system. It is reasonably certain that the *thalamus* and the *hypothalamus*, as well as the *basal ganglia* which form the last layer before the ultimate or top layer of the cerebral cortex, are all under the control of the cerebral cortex. It is certain, in any event, that they work in close harmony with the controlling areas of the cerebral cortex in providing the integrated behaviour of the person. Discussion of these various controlling centres, particularly the lower reflex centres, and their relationship to the control of internal body-states (body temperature, blood-pressure, etc.) goes far beyond the compass of the present book. The *cerebral cortex* represents the controlling centre of all behavioural activities in man and it is this complex layer of nerve cells which has been the centre of most recent psychological and physiological investigation.

The problem of understanding human behaviour lies in filling the gap between observable stimulus and observable response; whatever else happens between stimulus and response, it is certain that the cerebral cortex plays a vital part.

The evidence comes from destruction (by either experiment or accident) of various parts of the cerebral cortex and is of special interest. To describe it briefly a simple map will help. The cortex is divided into four areas: the frontal areas constitute most of the front half of the top of the brain; the temporal areas around the ear, and slightly above it; the parietal areas on top of the head and top sides, roughly in the centre of the head; and the occipital areas, constituting the area covered at the back of the head.

The cerebral cortex, which forms the bulk of observable surface of the exposed brain, looks something like a very large walnut and is symmetrical in two hemispheres joined by connecting association fibres. Each of the four areas is duplicated, one on each side; the areas themselves are isolated from each other by some of the more obvious crevices (called fissures) which are clearly visible on the surface of the brain. It is of special interest to consider what happens when any of these is either damaged or electrically stimulated. The occipital areas are at the back of the head and specifically concerned with vision; destruction of the cortex in the occipital areas leads to partial or complete blindness. The occipital area is concerned with the primary and secondary visual areas; the areas of visual elaboration, which are thought to be interpretive and therefore probably concerned with perception, are forward of the primary areas. The eyes are the main source of sensory input; the majority of the information the human being receives is through the eyes, although much of this information *could* be picked up through the ears or other senses; this is what happens to the blind.

The eyes have important connections with the brain. These connections are the optical nervous pathways, starting at the retina—a thin nerve layer, made up principally of rods and cones in the back of the eye. They run back to the *optic chiasma*, where part of the fibre tracts cross over, and then, after certain connections with the thalamus, they run back to the occipital areas. The crossing-over of nerve fibres is typical of much of the nervous system: the right arm and leg are controlled from the left hemisphere of the cerebral cortex and the left arm and leg from the right hemisphere. Indeed, the left side of the body is generally controlled by the right hemisphere, and vice-versa. Right-handed people are left-hemisphere dominants. The occipital lobe is, except for the speech areas of the brain, probably the most specific in function of the whole of the cortical regions.

The speech areas are on the side of the brain. Various forms of speech defect, known collectively as *aphasia*, occur with damage of the speech areas. The primary speech areas are in the superior, or upper frontal, area and in both the temporal and parietal areas. Destruction of the speech areas may lead to many different sorts of disorders: loss of speech, loss of various uses of words, loss of association of word and object, and so on. These are areas where sign and symbol activities are stored, and might well have been called the 'semantic areas'.

The temporal areas are closely connected with memory, as well as containing areas serving both audition and equilibrium. Direct electrical stimulation of the temporal areas results in reports of visual scenes from the patient's past. It is important that we discover as much as possible about the location of memory, since, as with the digital computer, it is the extent of, and accessibility of, the memory which determines, to a great extent, the abilities of the organism. Illusions and hallucinations are also closely connected with this area. Electrical stimulation of this area can completely bewilder the patient about the present state of his surrounding. The belief is that more stable neural patterns exist in this temporal part of the cortex than any other. The synaptic connections, if these are indeed the foundation of 'learning', are probably of a relatively permanent fashion in this area. The parietal lobe, which lies on top of the head and on its upper sides, is not very revealing and, like the frontal lobe, does not respond markedly to electrical stimulation. However, on removal of most of the parietal cortex in the non-dominant hemisphere, the arm on the opposite side is affected, so that when the patient dresses, he makes no use of his opposite (left) arm and acts just as if he is unaware of its presence. The parietal areas are connected with mental projection of the opposite limb.

The hemispheres of the brain are usually divided into dominant and non-dominant hemispheres and these may vary for different people. It is probable that the whole cerebral cortex involves a mapping of all the systems of the person and subserves most of his functions. The relation between the areas, however, may be complex. Certainly the areas overlap, and the interrelated threshold values (sensitivity of nerve cells to stimulation) change differentially with changes of movement by the individual.

The notion of threshold deserves more detailed consideration. If a nerve fibre is stimulated, then it will respond if the stimulus is sufficiently strong, but it is possible to stimulate a fibre and receive no response. The *threshold* is the point where a fibre responds to the minimal stimulus; it is a measure of the sensitivity of any neuron or collection of neurons.

In the cerebral cortex, in which an overlap of representation takes place, stimulation of a single point will elicit one or other function according to the relative thresholds of the particular functions controlled by that particular point.

The frontal lobe of the cerebral cortex, which is closely related to consciousness, self-consciousness and imagination, has caused the greatest interest, because here a considerable amount of destruction can take place without, apparently, affecting much of the overt behaviour of the individual. Those changes which occur are mainly changes in the person's personality. A brief example will show a typical response to removal of large parts of the frontal lobes. A man, previously shy and retiring, with 'frustrating states' was operated on, and the frontal areas were partially destroyed. At first he seemed to have recovered completely. Soon, however, his friends reported marked changes in habits: no more shyness, but a gay disregard for conventions and money. His 'frustration' had gone and, with it, any sense of planning, social organization or responsibility; the two had gone together.

Among the basic ideas of these neurological experiments and the subsequent models is the notion of a *reflex arc*. The reflex arc is a simple cybernetic model of the mechanisms of the human nervous system.

Experiments which have contributed so much to the reflex arc theory include electrical stimulation of muscle-nerve preparations; a typical piece of muscle is removed from a frog's leg, and with it go its attached nerve fibres. Sir Charles Sherrington was one of the founders of the reflex-arc theory. He developed a fairly complex theory of neural functioning in which he used to describe his hypothetical mechanism in terms such as 'central excitatory state', 'central inhibitory state'. He demonstrated processes of both inhibition and facilitation of a nerve impulse. Indeed, he supplied a picture of impulses travelling down nerves, rather in the same manner as trains travel along many lines, or messages travel along a telephone network.

If two trains are running along parallel lines which meet, it is obviously necessary to stop one train and let it through first to inhibit or stop the passage of the other train. When the impulses are not antagonistic—since both may carry on together reinforcing one another—one train is hooked onto the other, making a bigger train. Sometimes circumstances arise so that no train can pass at all unless both the component trains arrive together. In terms of our analogy, trains of five carriages (and no more) must use the lines up to the junction, while all trains after the junction must have at least ten carriages, so we must have two trains coming up together. The central excitatory and inhibitory states refer to whether or not the junction box allows trains through—

'its signal is down' or 'not down', which implies 'signal up'. Of course, the picture is really more complex than this, but we shall use this basic knowledge of the way nerve fibres behave when we construct our neural networks. This is a simple cybernetic model.

The E.E.G. (or electro-encephalograph) is an instrument for measuring the electrical activity of the brain between two points where the electrodes are placed. The best-known characteristic is that of the alpha-rhythm which occurs when a person at rest closes his eyes. It is of special interest because it is thought that this alpha-rhythm is associated with the steady scanning rhythm of the visual mechanism. This is what is used in television, and the resemblance between television and human vision is one that suggests the very development of cybernetics with which we are concerned.

The work done recently on the E.E.G. has been on such a large scale that it would take too long a time to discuss. Perhaps the principal points to mention are that the electrical records so far collected indicate the strong interrelation existing between the electrical state of the organism and the chemical and other states. At the same time, the most general hypothesis derived from E.E.G. work is that there is a sort of homeostatic process governing the electrical activity, in much the same way as there is a homeostatic principle governing most, if not all, of behaviour. So perception is regarded as the process of scanning the visual field for sensory stimuli, and the analogy of television must, perforce, somewhat modify our picture of the nervous system. No longer is it just a telephone switchboard system, but a complex computer involving the encoding and decoding of messages passing through. This is not by any means inconsistent with the idea of a telephonic system, but is rather more complex than the type of telephone system which might immediately occur to us.

Let us now briefly discuss localization of function in the cerebral cortex. In rats, at least, cortical destruction, irrespective of the location in the cortex, seems to have the same effect on learning. Professor D. O. Hebb finds that the difficulty this implies for specific functioning is avoidable if it is seen that destruction of part of a neural network does not necessarily lead to loss of the associated function; rather it is a short-circuiting which permits the associated function to be retained.

The cell assembly theory is closely connected with the long-held classical view that the nervous system must make new connections at the synaptic junction. There now exists some evidence for the presence of such synaptic knobs (which increase with age) during the period of early development. It has been suggested that a 'phase-sequence' occurs in the brain while scanning a figure or shape. This ordered phase-sequence permits, if suitable repetitions are made, the setting up of new networks, helped possibly by slight neural growth. Hebb uses this to allow the time for the necessary neural growth, which leads to the composition of the new network.

It is difficult, in a short chapter, to illustrate the depth and complexity of the subject of changes in the brain as we learn, but at least it looks likely that changes of behaviour are accompanied by changes in brain connections; we think of such changes as the result of growth.

The cybernetic importance of physiology is much the same as its importance to psychology. This is inevitable because, of course, we are thinking of physiology and psychology as essentially the same subject; the cybernetician, being interested in modelling, learning and feedback systems, is naturally interested in the behaviour and mechanisms of the human brain.

The importance of physiology is, of course, that it describes forms of natural control and communication systems, and this allows us to understand human behaviour. There are a variety of ways in which we may use this information, but the most obvious way is in the simulation of human behaviour. But for synthesis too, our knowledge of possible physiological changes is of the utmost importance.

We are back with our 'black box'. We know what it does, and we can predict, by external observation alone, its behaviour with some accuracy. But for the more detailed prediction demanded by psychologists, the 'internal' physiological details are necessary. It is like looking at a car. Up to a point you can predict and understand its performance without looking under the bonnet, but beyond that point it is hopeless, especially when the engine stops.

Cybernetics supplies models at the detailed physiological level as at the broader psychological level. In doing so, it has mainly modelled the nervous system in a subject now called neurocybernetics.

SUMMARY

Physiology, especially neuro-physiology, is concerned with discovering the mechanisms developed in evolution, and used by human beings.

The central nervous system divides into the brain and the grey matter (nerve cells) of the spinal cord. The brain itself divides up into areas like telephone exchanges in a telephone network. The headquarters is the cerebral cortex which is finally responsible for controlling all the activities of the human being.

This is a matter of opening the black box, which is an example of a natural control and communication system.

CHAPTER TEN
MANAGEMENT CYBERNETICS

ARGUMENT

Cybernetics cuts across the established sciences and dips into each, extracting what is common to communication and control, and capable of being dealt with in the dynamic terms of feedback.

Management Cybernetics is precisely one such case in which cybernetics overlaps the problems of management science.

The resulting mixture involves heuristic methods, decision procedures, computers and Operational Research.

Cybernetic Management

Cybernetics is also the science of management, and, in some senses, the science of science. It contains the fundamental ingredients needed for all of organization and planning. The word cybernetics applies, as we have said frequently, to any sort of closed-loop system which is adaptive; commercial enterprises and all types of business *should* be that.

A commercial enterprise can be likened to a human body: it needs a brain to control it. To achieve effective control requires eyes, ears and the other senses to pick up details of the environment. This refers especially to *changes* in the environment, and at this point we should be reminded of the importance of 'management by exception'—that is, the need for control where change occurs. Change is vital and creates the need for control; communication tells the brain when and where to exercise that control.

A business or industry, like an individual, needs to anticipate events. So sales estimating, market research, motivational research, accountancy records and advertising anticipate and attempt to pave the way for a successful business. We know what to make and how to make it, or what to store and how much of it to store, only if we can successfully anticipate future demands. This is like the behaviour of an intelligent person and, just as we lay plans as individuals, so any management group must plan for the success of its company. This process of planning forms a major part of cybernetics. The communication part is obvious and the control—not in any totalitarian sense of the word—is meant in a common sense manner.

The basic idea of Management Cybernetics is that a business is like a human being. It needs a brain to *control* it. To carry out that control effectively requires eyes, ears and the other special senses, in order to pick up information. This, as we have said, refers especially to *changes* in the environment.

Cybernetics also caters for decision-making under conditions of uncertainty due to incomplete information. The methods are usually mathematical or statistical, often complicated, and often requiring a computer to put them into practice; but the results can be far better than even the best executive can achieve unaided. Business is something for human beings, which taxes their intelligence and their ability to assess people and situations. Now, whether we like it or not, the world of the amateur planner is giving way to the world of the professional, or scientific, planner and the professional depends more and more on the technique of modern science; cybernetics provides precisely the *science* of management, under the name of Management Cybernetics.

Operational Research, Computer Science, Organization and Method, Work Study and many other techniques all play their part, and vital parts they are, but in the end it is the science of control and communication which provides the basis upon which they all operate. In a large or a small company, information is received from many sources, and different groups supply and sieve the information. These different groups have different vested interests and biases and present their information accordingly. Senior management sifts this information and tries to reach agreement about action which would be in the best interests of the company. All of this can be made more efficient by knowledge of the processes involved, by use of techniques which may be complex but whose arms are easy to understand and easy to use, by having information sources made easily available and by following a cybernetic line of approach.

In Management Cybernetics there are two main factors under consideration. The first is very general and refers to the attitude to be adopted, and the second is quite specific and refers to the methods to be used. As far as the first is concerned we have to say that it is in some sense intangible; you have to believe that a system, such as a business or a government, is like an organism and is capable of being controlled by a 'brain'. The 'brain' is the Board of Directors, or the Government itself, and must act in a regulating capacity. What needs to be spelled out is that human brains in individuals and Boards of Directors in companies can be similar. This is not to say that the artificial brain cannot control its system more efficiently than the human brain controls its body; the point is, rather, that if the Board can approach the capacity of the human brain and can also evolve with experience, then it can take full advantage of its ability to make it so.

Now to the more particular strategies and tactics. For the sake of exposition we shall assume you are a military commander in a war (rather than a business man at peace, although the way one method could be used in the other context should be fairly obvious). You are in command of combined forces engaged in a major battle of the kind that often occurred in World War II. You have advanced overland and captured an important land base—a city of great strategic importance. You apparently have (relative) control of the sea and, although you are uncertain about the air power, you are clear that if you are to win the war you have to push forward and take further enemy bases on the way into the enemy stronghold.

You need to take decisions now: you could attack immediately or you could delay in order to regroup your forces, making them more efficient as a result. As a cybernetician, you will now analyze the situation, in which you find yourself, in terms of motive and purpose, ends and means, and you will necessarily do it in probabilistic terms. It is clear that the enemy wants to beat you and you must know something about the deployment and strength of his forces.

The first question which arises is: was his retreat the result of our driving him back, an orderly retreat, a bluff, or just to strengthen his defensive position? Geographical factors and historical factors play a part in your assessment here, and the use of *heuristics* is most relevant. We must now explain what we mean by heuristic methods.

Heuristic Methods

Two contrasting ways of carrying out any operation are illustrated by heuristics or algorithms. An algorithm is a precise means for arriving at a definite solution to a well-defined problem. If you are asked how many men there are in a room, the answer is found by counting them. The method is precise and the solution clear. This is an algorithm at work.

If you have a situation, such as a game of chess, where you do *not* know the 'best' move to make at any point of the game, you invoke general principles such as 'control the centre of the board', 'exchange pieces if it is to your advantage', etc . . . 'to your advantage' is vague because you may get the better of the immediate exchange of the pieces and yet lose in terms of overall position. These methods are heuristic. Good heuristics are valuable short cuts or guides and, if we carefully record their use and the results of their use, we can steadily improve and make them more precise. Using scientific methods we can, sometimes, even turn heuristics into algorithms. All of this is rather like saying that we can remove the uncertainty in a situation by increasing our knowledge of it. In a sense this is a truism; in practice it presents a challenge.

Methods for providing off-line adaptive models or

simulations and superimposing heuristic programs with language and logical facilities are of the utmost importance in commercial computer applications. This whole field is closely bound up with existing methods of systems analysis and conventional computer programming. It is part of an attempt to provide overall computer control of any system whatever—be it commercial, academic, industrial or governmental. The complete plan will also involve an integrated approach to process and production control.

The first step in the conventional programming of a computer involves providing an overall block diagram, or flow chart, of the principal features of the system (e.g. the whole of a company). The second step is to provide a point of departure which demands a conventional systems analysis of some sub-system or section of the total system. We should normally start with a section dealing with scheduling, planning, or some such activity, which is both centrally placed in the system, and convenient, for further analysis, as a spreading point. Such an approach can and must be made coherent with any existing data processing system, even though, or even especially where, payroll and other well-established computer methods are already in use.

During the first stage of the operation one must tackle the whole problem of compatibility, choice of suitable computer and suitable computer language (whether to use PL1, COBOL, ALGOL, FORTRAN or machine code) and integration from an overall vantage point. This must, of course, include the search for compatibility and plans for ultimate integration of process control with production control and planning.

The next point is vital and concerns the need for 're-thinking'. Having all conventional techniques such as linear and dynamic programming available, and thinking of our undertaking as involving an overall modelling, then to rethink our purpose is quite central and vital. The modelling uses, in the main, logico-mathematical methods, and treats any system as being evolutionary. The emphasis, in other words is on modelling and controlling a *changing* system. This implies the need for adaptive and dynamic forms of models.

Heuristic Programming

Granted acceptance of conventional systems analysis and programming, and granted agreement on the aforesaid philosophy, we now proceed to the stage of heuristic programming. Heuristics are 'general rules of thumb' or *ad hoc* principles applied in situations where algorithms (detailed precise automatic procedures) cannot be applied for reasons of either economy or inherent difficulties. Playing chess provides an example involving economy, while sales estimation, since it implies future unknown states (incomplete information), has inherent difficulties. A heuristic in chess, as we said earlier, might be 'always control the centre of the board'.

In commercial and industrial systems, heuristics, such as 'exponential smoothing' usually supply such rough guides to future demand. Sales models, often supplemented by market and motivational research, supply heuristics for marketing purposes.

Although one- or two-way interrogation in the computer can be wholly independent of heuristics, the very fact that heuristics are essentially linguistic, especially in the form of inductive generalizations, suggests a close relationship. Language is superimposed upon our conventionally constructed model. The object is to permit easy communications between programmer (or an executive, who need know nothing of computing) and the computer.

At this stage, questions and statements to the computer form the one-way linguistic transaction which permits easy data retrieval. At present, questions have to be in stylized English, and are limited as to their domain of operation, but may soon be more nearly universal. The plan is to have a verbal description, supplemented by data, over a domain, e.g. the supply section of a company. This process is selective and quickly elicits answers, by verbal discourse, to pertinent questions.

Logical inference is now used to supplement the data retrieval search: for example, if one asks how much the company spent on a raw material, say, during May, the computer may infer the answer from knowing the figure for April and also knowing that the April figure was the same as May's. This obviously trivial example illustrates a technique which can be made extremely powerful. This form of programming also suggests setting up axiomatic model-systems for marketing, etc: they allow one to draw probable inferences, which, when supplemented by empirical data—from surveys and the like—give a clear and useful model of some aspect of the total system.

This is as far as we shall take this argument, since to set up even a relatively simple evolutionary model, where it is assumed that the models can be made adaptive, and the heuristics themselves are obviously capable of being adaptive, is a time-consuming process, although it is a necessary step to the computerization of decision making.

Let us next look again at our hypothetical military commander. The commander who is assessing his enemy's behaviour should regard such matters as vital. He may have a heuristic which says 'Commanders never withdraw voluntarily, or as a bluff, at certain times of the year, because a change of weather will occur which makes it vital to hold every yard'. If such a heuristic can be invoked, then a probability of a fairly high value (near certainty) can be ascribed to his reasons for retreat: he was forced to.

The drawing of logical inference clearly enters into decision-taking, so we may now say 'then he is in some disarray, since forced retreat is a source of chaos'. We therefore look for evidence of chaos, which confirms our heuristic, and helps to determine our next move. Another heuristic may now be invoked 'If you are following a retreating army which is in disarray, harry them to the limits'. By this time, our commander is ordering, after his first reconnaissance flights, an attack by air, and preparing his troops for immediate advance.

But now there is a further consideration. So far our commander has thought only in terms of *probable* enemy activity. What is the state of his own forces? They are tired, but capable of the job provided he is right that the enemy is not bluffing. The question he should now ask is 'what will be the result of our attack if the enemy *is* bluffing?' The answer may be 'complete defeat for us'. In other words, he is taking a great risk and should consider a second strategy. 'What happens if I rest at my new position and consolidate it, and bring up some reserve troops?', and so the analysis continues. It is rather like a chess player weighing the alternatives, using common sense and logic. Cybernetics is precisely the process, in its decision-taking role, of insisting on the use of common sense and logic. There are, though, two factors which make the cybernetician rather different from the usual decision-taker. These are that he makes his arguments *explicit* and allows the detail to be checked and verified, which allows him to use a computer for his purpose.

The commander with insight accumulates his experience, but finds it difficult to hand his experience on to others because it has not been made explicit; he has, therefore, called his decision-making process a hunch or 'having a nose for things', 'smelling a rat', etc. But this *can* all be made explicit and then becomes much more powerful.

Management Cybernetics in Practice

Let us now look at another example. Imagine yourself in a board meeting and imagine the need to make a decision whether or not to take over another company. You want to know what the new company's profits are, you want to know the profit margins in the trade, and you also want to know all sorts of details about their past results, present state and plans. All you have to do is say 'What are . . .', finish the sentence appropriately and the secretary types out the question on the typewriter which is 'on line' with the computer system. The question does not even need to be in specially selected phrases, and the secretary need not translate or code it; indeed you can type the question yourself in ordinary English and wait only a few seconds to read the typed answer. This is all made possible by what is called natural language programming. We shall discuss this shortly.

If you ask a question which is not merely a matter of fact but a matter for logical inference or statistical analysis, then the whole situation becomes more complicated. Now the computer has to perform the necessary analysis—whether mathematical, logical or statistical—so it may be a minute or so before the answer is available. But this compares with an hour or two if you use a human mathematician.

Such methods, which form an important part of cybernetics, provide ways of streamlining the whole decision-making process; it does not matter whether facts or inferences from facts are needed, the result is the same. The only thing that is different is that one takes longer than the other.

The technique of natural language programming on a

computer is closely related to another field of heuristic programming. Heuristic programs, as we have said, deal with planning, decision taking and risk. Just as people can play business games, so the computer can be programmed to play much more realistic and more complicated business games; and it does so in a fraction of the time that a human being would take. It also produces better results.

Even if your information is incomplete and you have to include guesses and estimates—even of people's trustworthiness or other facets of their character—this can be done by using heuristic methods.

One reason for the great power involved in heuristic methods is the fact that human beings, for all their flexibility and brilliance, cannot easily assess and evaluate a whole set of factors which refer to a complex situation; but a mathematical model can enable the computer to do this and do it at many thousands of times the speed of the human being. Imagine the human analysis of every possible board state for each of two consecutive moves in chess; almost completely beyond a human being, but a computer could point out each possible board state in a matter of minutes, at most.

Mathematical methods play a vital part. There are various forms of decision processing such as those involved in the rules of probability; you may assess the probability of some event and act accordingly, or combine the probabilities for various possible events with the *desirabilities*, and combine them to find a 'best' decision. Here you may be prepared to take a risk on the probabilities for the sake of the desirabilities.

Let us look at what is called Risk Analysis. You are asked to place a bet on some event such as a horse or a dog race. If the amount involved is only £1, you may not bother about losing, and place the money on an outsider. The reason is that you are risking very little and if you are wrong, you will have little cause for regret.

If the amount involved in the bet were £1,000 you may feel quite differently, and invoke all sorts of ways of defraying your losses; you may hedge your bet, or distribute it amongst the favourites. Now your risk is great and your regret, if you are wrong, can be very great.

In the case of our commander taking military decisions, or in the case of political decision-taking—minimizing regret (or minimizing risk under circumstances of great threat) is as important as weighing the probabilities of events in the first place. It is easy to see in these circumstances how strategies can range from complete optimism to complete pessimism. The requirement is an assessment of an assessment and must take *all* the *relevant* facts into consideration.

It is, at this stage, the man-machine relationship which is so vital. A man works with a computer so that the computer shows off its speed, accuracy and ability to handle complex material, while the human being uses his flexibility and his gift for quick insight and sense of relevance. But as time goes by, more and more will the man-machine phase of development be replaced by the machine phase. This is simply because we, as human beings, can develop a machine evolution far more quickly than a human evolution. We cannot easily enlarge our brains and, although we can perhaps make more use of them, by improving our educational techniques—and this cybernetics hopes to help to do—even so our ingenuity is given even more scope in programming larger and larger computers.

We shall now say a few words about natural language programming, since this is closely related to heuristic methods, especially those of the non-numerical kind.

Natural Language Programming

Natural language programming is concerned with an

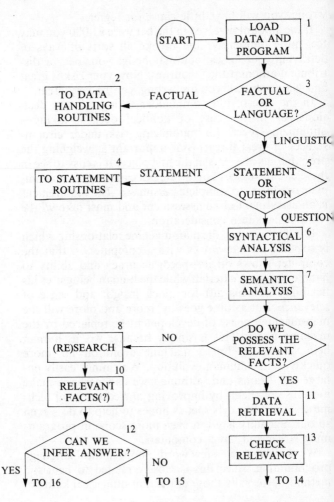

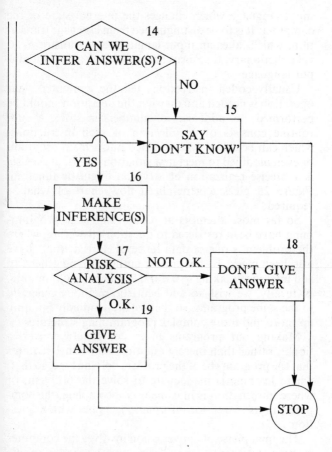

Figure 23
This flow chart shows the essential process of answering a question
under conditions of inference-making and risk.

input language which changes the internal state of the computer. It is to be distinguished from language translation, which takes an input language and transforms it, via a dictionary, thesaurus and sets of rules, into an output language.

Usually coded instructions tell the computer what operation is needed and on what the operation should be performed, i.e. addresses of numbers in store. A subroutine consists of a collection of such instructions, which can be called up and edited into a main program, or even modified to meet new situations. This, in a sense, is a precise realization of a typical linguistic function. Figure 23 gives a generalized flow chart of what is required.

So far most attempts at natural language programming have been restricted to question-answering, where the problem is one of data retrieval. But attempts have also been made, by the present author among others, to add inference-making to natural language programming. Naturally, we wish to add heuristic methods generally to the same programs, so that we are gradually building up more and more complex programming structures.

Making our programs more completely conversational, rather than merely question-answering, requires that the programs be of the problem-solving type, so that, where learning is inadequate to solve the problem, or where information is in some way incomplete, the computer, in its search for information, replies with a question.

The final phase of conversation involves the computer making statements for the same sort of reason people make statements, namely to change someone's views or to persuade them to do something. This implies the inclusion of models or simulations of social situations which the computer must need to control or direct. This is easy enough in principle but must be one that any organisation, which believes the computerized company to be the company of the future, should be initiating. We shall now say a few last words about the importance of selecting relevant information for the benefit of management decision-taking.

Selecting Relevant Information

Both large and small companies receive information from many different sources: large numbers of people hold, supply and sort information. These people have different vested interests and biases, and present their information accordingly. Management itself appraises this information and attempts to reach agreement as to what action would be in the best interests of the company. All of this can be made very much more efficient by knowing the processes involved, by using techniques which may be complex but are easy to use, by having information sources made readily available and in general by following a cybernetic line of approach.

Computers generate a great bulk of paper in the form of computer output. The judicious computer manager ensures that the output is in readable form and does not, if he can help it, overload the receiver. In practice, this approach produces tables and other data that leave the executive confused. The result is very rarely effective. Cybernetics does it very differently. It assumes the Board wants to know only what is relevant to a particular problem.

Relevancy is the essence of the whole problem. It is all too easy, as every director knows, to swamp his Board and his management with useless information. The uselessness stems from many factors: sheets of tabulations are not easy to follow, and whereas one can read the data it is difficult to relate that data to the relevant considerations under review. This is one reason for the development of natural language programs.

Management Cybernetics is a very important part of cybernetic development, and one that we can expect to progress at a great rate in the future.

There are many aspects of this fast-developing subject that we have no space to consider. But we can at least list the following headings which should be followed up by those interested:

1. Corporate business strategies.
2. Company models.
3. Cash flow (and other) models of the company.
4. Models for diversification, expansion, acquisition and investment.
5. Decision taking, planning and problem solving by individuals and groups.
6. The analysis of individual and group behaviour, especially under conditions of decision taking, planning and problem solving.
7. Economic models.
8. Marketing models.
9. Motivational models.

SUMMARY

Management Cybernetics is concerned with methods of planning, decision-taking and problem-solving. Sometimes the methods used are common sense, mathematics and statistics, but more often computers and models are required to simulate complex situations.

The prime need in Management Cybernetics is to recognize the dynamic nature of reality, where that reality is the business environment or the market place. It is necessary, therefore, that models should be adaptive and heuristic.

Natural language programming fits nicely into the heuristic picture, together with various techniques for evaluating data, such as Risk Analysis.

We have tried to show some fairly practical examples of these methods.

CHAPTER ELEVEN
CYBERNETICS AND EDUCATION

ARGUMENT

It is natural that cybernetics should be involved in all the major features of society. Educational Cybernetics is not yet the title used for this field, but no doubt in time it will become so.

The main role of cybernetics in education is to supply a feedback type of system, and this is particularly appropriate in a form which requires teaching machines or computers for its presentation. These fields are called Programmed Instruction (P.I.) and Computer Assisted Instruction (C.A.I.) respectively.

We would expect such methods to be used, in the future, within the context of schools, universities and every other type of training organization.

Introduction

Cybernetics in education can obviously apply to the organisation of an educational system. Computers and heuristic methods are necessary for the organisation of the new type of flexible education system required at all levels of the existing educational system.

Needless to say, such a system should be both dynamic and adaptive and it should also, like management problems, involve heuristic methods.

Before we discuss the variations implied by heuristic methods, let us describe, in the simplest terms, the methods commonly used in programmed instruction, or programmed learning as it is sometimes called.

Programmed Instruction

Programmed instruction is the general name for the field of teaching machines, programmed books and computer assisted instruction. It refers to the method of writing the programmes rather than their method of presentation.

The use of the word 'programmed' emphasizes that the method provides feedback to the learner. It is therefore unlike most other sources of instructional communication between people. The television, the radio, the lecture, even the class-room teacher, act as a source of information without receiving any immediate feedback from those being taught. In radio and television, of course, this is impossible in their ordinary use, and even in the case of the lecturer or teacher very little feedback tends to occur in practice. This is because a lack of understanding on the part of the student cannot modify how they are taught or what they are taught. Programmed instruction, on the other hand, proceeds on a step by step basis, using the question and immediate answer technique as a feedback link to modify, according to his performance, the student's subsequent behaviour.

Programmed instruction breaks down information on a step by step basis and ask questions about that information; it then supplies answers. The student reading the text, whether from machine or book, cannot proceed to the next frame of the programme without having at least learned the correct answer to the question posed on the last frame. It is hoped that he also understands what he is told, but this cannot be guaranteed.

Historically, programmed instruction goes back to the work of English (1918) who taught, by such methods, British army recruits how to use the rifle. His work was based on a principle extremely similar to that used in current *linear* type programmes. In 1926 and the following years, Professor Pressey, at Ohio State University in the U.S.A., made teaching machines and used programmed instruction for teaching various subjects.

Pressey's work involved both the construction of experimental machines and experimental work with programmes in book form. These experimental books included both the direct question, whether in 'sentence completion form' or otherwise, and the multiple-choice question. So far as the multiple choice question was concerned, however, his use differed from modern versions, especially those used by Crowder, for he did not use separate frames for dealing with wrong answers.

By a direct question, we mean, of course, something like 'Who killed Cock Robin?'; this question could be put in sentence completion form as '. . . killed Cock Robin?' and it is the student's problem to fill in the blank. In the multiple choice form, we find the direct question as before with a series of alternative answers: 1. Alice in Wonderland; 2. The Sparrow; 3. Tiger Tim. The student must choose which answer he thinks to be correct and turn to the relevant page or frame. He will then be told if he is right or wrong; if he is wrong, he will either be told to go back, think again about it, and re-

read what has been said, or he may be sent on to a new frame or page containing new information relevant to the original question which will eventually return him to that question.

The recent rediscovery of programmed instruction dates back some fourteen years, to approximately 1956. Work on the computer, and the general development of automation, coupled with awareness that the number of teachers was decreasing at a time when the demand for them was increasing, led to the manufacture of new teaching machines, the writing of new programmes and the publication of new programmed books. The development of a whole new technology of education.

We shall now distinguish between the branching and linear methods as basic methods of writing programmes for teaching machines. Hybrid methods, mixing the two, are also used.

The Methods Used by Programmed Instruction

The basic and simplest method used in programming is to divide information into small blocks and then supply questions and answers linking each block (frames or pages) to the next.

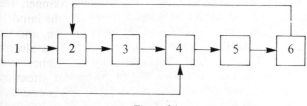

Figure 24

On each frame we have the answer to a previous question, a new piece of information and the next question; the next frame has the answer to the question on the last frame, more information and a new question and so on.

We can introduce skips, which take the student backward and forward according to whether he has failed to pass a test or already knows the information in some section of the complete programme. This leads to greater flexibility than is afforded by a straight piece of linear programming; it saves time and avoids boredom.

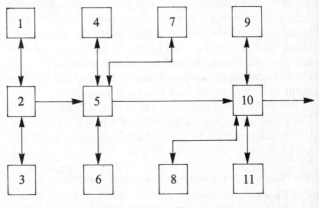

Figure 25

Linear programmes take various forms, but the one most usually associated with the origin of linear programming is associated with the name of Skinner. He used short frames and tended to emphasize the importance of conditioning the student by repetition, and by trying to ensure that the correct answer was always selected by the student. There is some evidence that Skinner's programmes did not pay sufficient attention to the so-called 'gradient of learning' which is essential to the good programme. It is very important that the programme should start relatively slowly and accumulate information while gathering momentum in the process. It is this 'gradient of learning' which must on the one hand cater for the average audience for whom the programme is intended, and yet have enough flexibility to deal with variations in the average rate of progress. Because there is a spread of abilities over which any programme must operate, branching methods are often felt to be more suitable. Norman Crowder is especially associated with the development of branching machines and branching programmes. Figure 25 shows an example of *simple branching*:

In the same simple branching programme where an answer is selected from a multiple-choice question, the frame answers immediately give some information which helps the student to deduce the reasons for being wrong, and also returns to the original question where he makes a new selection. This shows more variation than simple branching alone but is still not varied enough, even with various ranges of choice.

Complex branching (an example is shown in Figure 26) involves remedial sub-routes where the student is taken off the main route of the programme for more detailed remedial treatment and for the repetition of the original question in slightly modified form, using, for example, a different analogy or metaphor. It is important that remedial sub-routes will only be used for vitally important rules or principles which are essential in the total development of the programme.

It must be emphasized that the *planning* of programmes is an essential part of the programme writing process. This can be divided into various stages. It starts with the specification of the programme, which decides what age groups, what type of intelligence, what type of previous knowledge is assumed, etc., in the programme. This is accompanied by a pre-requisite test which tests for knowledge of the information presupposed and a pre-test which tests for knowledge actually given in the programme. Success in the pre-requisite test and failure in the pre-test are necessary conditions for

starting the programme. At the end of the programme
there is a post-test which is equivalent in difficulty to the
pre-test. Then, by comparison between the pre- and
post-test, some measures of the efficiency of the programme can be assessed. All of this helps us to improve
our methods of instruction.

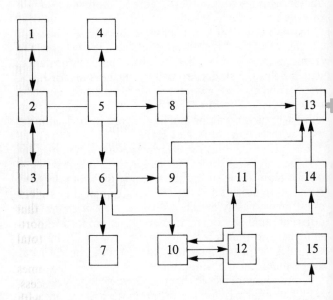

Figure 26

After the specification we come to the detailed planning of the programme. It is essential to make sure that
the concepts, the rules and all the information which the
programme is intended to transmit to the student is
organized down to the minutest detail. The order in
which the information is to be presented must be care-

fully considered and the planner must make up his own mind what the optimum order is. At the same time the planner must remind himself that in his programme he must cater for different levels of abstraction. In other words, he must set the general theme, explain why the person is being taught what he is being taught and, at each particular stage, the detail to be taught must be related to the plan of the programme as a whole. In other words, he may be learning a specific technique in the field of Operational Research for example, but he must understand what the whole of Operational Research is about in order to see how the particular detail of a technique relates to the whole of the subject.

Following on the detailed plan of the programme, the frames should be constrained to such an extent that almost anyone picking up the plan could write the frames without them being too different from those of any other frame writer. There are many 'tricks of the trade' in writing frames; one is not always telling the student whether he is right or wrong straight away, thus encouraging him to read the whole frame. He might otherwise guess or skip if he knew he were wrong or right immediately. There are many such tricks as this which are part and parcel of the stock-in-trade of the programme writer.

When completed, the programmes are tested and evaluated in some detail. They are tried out on a sample of the population for which they are intended; they are 'proof read' and read by specialists in the particular material content. In the end, when all corrections have been made, the programme can appear either in machine or book form, or both.

Contrasting machines and books, one can say straight away that, in general, experimental evidence has tended to favour the machine; but both have had some fair measure of success for there is reason to suppose that in ideal circumstances programmed instruction should be a central feature of every training course.

It may be assumed that each particular form has its own particular merits, and we shall not argue whether linear is better than branching or vice versa. We can, however, say one specific thing, and that is that mixed programmes which involve both branching and linear frames together are probably, by and large, the most efficient way of presenting information.

It might be argued that where a person is presenting a fair amount of factual information, which must be remembered and regurgitated by the student, the linear method has much to recommend it. Where the maximum amount of inference is to be made the branching method is probably more effective. It should always be remembered as a matter of overriding importance that, wherever possible, the good programmer will make the student do the maximum amount of work. This entails use of the method of discovery, where the student has to work out as much as he can for himself, and does not merely remember things that have been worked out for him.

So much then for our brief outline of the basic methods used in programmed instruction. We should add that we have no time to discuss serious modifications and variations on these basic techniques; nor do we have space to discuss the use of teaching machines for skilled non-verbal activities or of auditory teaching machines. The reader should bear in mind that we are trying to describe the most important basic ingredients of a subject which has enormously wide ramifications and many variations attached to it. This is true of all aspects of cybernetics.

Programmed Instruction Applications
One of the most exciting applications of programmed instruction, and one which played its part in its recent re-

discovery, is that of fault-finding on complicated apparatus. The branching format lends itself particularly well to this type of use; however complicated the apparatus, whether television set, car, or even aircraft, in principle it is possible to eliminate systematically all the alternatives at each stage of the attempted procedure. Such methods certainly have the effect of providing the means for an uninformed person to handle complicated apparatus, the details of which he need not fully understand.

More recently branching and linear techniques have been used for teaching subjects by *descriptive* methods. It follows, of course, that programmed instruction can be used to teach anything at all. At the same time, it is clear that subjects like mathematics, logic and operational research lend themselves especially well to the systematic treatment afforded by programmed instruction.

Programmed instruction has played a practical part in almost every aspect of modern industry. Not only have work study and operational research programmes been made available, but programmes of one kind and another have been used for training people in foreign languages (these are usually audio-visual), and training operators at the bench itself (here solely auditory programmes are often used).

Programmes are now being used for rather more remote things, such as storage of information, which can be retrieved as it is needed.

In particular, programmes have been used by various travel organisations. If a traveller is going to a particular country, such as Chile or China, it is possible for him to get the necessary programme dealing with those aspects of the country with which he is concerned. He can then work through it in his own time.

It is, of course, clear that the range of programmed instruction covers most subjects and it only remains to emphasize the special problems that surround the actual communication process.

We can say that whenever we are dealing with an organization with a large number of people spread out over the country, or even over different parts of the world, there is a special value in the use of programmed instruction. To avoid the queueing problem—waiting for enough necessary people to gather together to make up a course—and to avoid the physical fact of having to bring them together for such a course, it is an advantage to be able to write a programme and circulate it to the individuals wherever they may be. This may or may not be used as a precursor to a course which takes place at some later time. Where it is a precursor of such a course the main role of programmed instruction is to create a homogeneous group out of what would otherwise be a heterogeneous one.

What has been said has probably already made it clear that programmed instruction cannot be viewed as just another technique to be used in training. It is, of course, only one method of training; it should be viewed among other audio-visual techniques such as closed-circuit television, radio and, above all, it is not to be thought of as a panacea. However, having said that, it seems likely, by virtue of its immediate feedback of results alone, to prove to be the central ingredient of any training or educational system of the future.

The problem now is how to make it most effective; like the computer, it cannot just be added to a system into which it does not fit; it must be a central feature. It is probably best to eliminate the idea that any sort of group instruction, whether or not in the class-room, is to be the basic ingredient of the training process. If the basic information is to be transmitted by programmed instruction (mainly in the form of teaching machines and programmes) and the human teacher, relieved from the burden of having to meet some syllabus deadline, plays the part of the tutor. In this way he uses his time far more efficiently, dealing with the individual difficulties arising in the course of working through programmes, or in the other features of any good training corps. In other words, discussion groups, television viewing and radio listening—together with all the other activities, including lectures and a certain amount of class-room work—will be basic to any training system; the tutor's ability to deal with individual problems will range over all these particular aspects under his control. We now take a brief look at C.A.I.

Computer Assisted Instruction (C.A.I.)

This involves the same basic principles involved in the rest of programmed learning, but now we have the information—on film in the teaching machines, or on the pages of the programmed text—centralized in the store of the computer.

By using computer terminals and multi-programming 'third generation' computers, we can provide on the screen of the terminal all the necessary information. The student behaves precisely as he does in the ordinary programmed learning situation. The only difference now is that the computer can keep a complete record of his behaviour as far as button-pressing choice is concerned. This fact alone makes C.A.I. particularly convenient for the validation of programmed texts, where by 'validation' we mean the careful testing and assessment of a programme to see that it does exactly what is intended.

C.A.I. has also the great advantage of being able to process a whole group of people, such as a class or even a whole school, and can deal with many different subjects at the same time provided the computer store is sufficiently large and there are enough terminals available.

A fair number of such systems exist in the U.S.A. There

are two at the University of Illinois called PLATO and SOCRATES. Such systems might be particularly appropriate in a modern educational establishment. Under such circumstances a large C.A.I. system could be used primarily for testing, organizing and tutoring, but perhaps not primarily for teaching. The reason teaching, for the moment, is probably best left to teaching machines or programmed books is an economic one. But if an expensive computer working at high speed is used for reference purposes, so that the bulk of students are looking up books, going through other programs and the like, then the C.A.I. system can be used to control a far greater number of students. At the same time *some* of these students can be actively taught on line by such a system.

This sort of view of a cybernetic school, as it were, bears on C.A.I. itself as the central ingredient, and can also make use of every kind of technical aid such as films, radio, television and computers.

The principles involved in this rethinking of education are essentially cybernetic; they emphasize feedback and automatic control of those features of education which are, because of their rather dull repetitive nature, best administered by machine. This has the effect of releasing many human beings from work best suited to machines and enables them to be used for work best done by humans. Here tutoring is the most obvious example.

We shall say no more about the cybernetic aspects of education, but the reader will appreciate that here, as in many other examples we have used, we have done little more than scratch the surface of the subject.

SUMMARY
Educational Cybernetics is a phrase only recently coined
to describe what is included in this chapter. Educational
Cybernetics deals with the technological features of an
educational system, primarily with the information
processing aspects, but this also implies methods for
feedback and control.

In this chapter we have described branching and linear
programming formats, and explained that these can be
used on teaching machines, in books or in the form of
Computer Assisted Instruction.

The question and answer and the subsequent approval
or correction provides the feedback loop; we have said
something about the applications of programmed
instruction both in educational establishments and
industry.

CHAPTER TWELVE
THE FUTURE OF CYBERNETICS

ARGUMENT

Cybernetics is concerned with dynamic systems. It is concerned with change and adaption to change.

This book has been concerned with trying to show the basic philosophy of cybernetics and some of its most important applications. The applications chosen are in behaviour theory, biology, education and management science. The principles involved are those of simulation, synthesis, adaption through feedback and the formulation of heuristics or hypotheses.

The results hold out the promise of being able to copy the whole of human rational abilities, and ultimately, no doubt, to improve on them.

Cybernetics has been defined in various equivalent ways and we should now be quite clear that we are dealing with problems of communication and control.

There are at least two sides to the subject. One is abstract, mathematico-logical in form and concerned with artificial intelligence. The other is applied, and deals with the application of cybernetics to all sorts of characteristic problems. Such problems include those of modelling human behaviour, modelling the nervous system, modelling industry and commerce, modelling the economy and modelling the educational system.

We have concentrated on a sample of these applications and have dealt with behaviour (psychology), the nervous system (neuro-physiology) and Management Cybernetics—which combines all the industrial applications. We have also discussed educational aspects of cybernetics, and this primarily means programmed learning and Computer Assisted Instruction.

On the 'pure' side of the subject, we have dealt with logic, automata theory, computers and information theory. These are the features which form the basis for the applications which we have described as cybernetics.

Two questions arise and should be answered now: 1. What other aspects of cybernetics exist apart from those already mentioned? 2. What is the likely future development of cybernetics?

The first question is answered in terms of decision processes such as Bayes Theorem, Minimax Regret and other methods which are designed to provide the pre-processing of information prior to the final act of decision taking.

Two central features of artificial intelligence are natural language programming and inference-making on computers. We have mentioned both of these developments, and here we should mention that these are two fields likely to develop rapidly in the future. The same is also true of all the various decision-making processes and models, as well as concept and hypothesis formation. All these features have been mentioned but we have made no attempt to provide a description in any detail.

The result is that we can look at the human being as a rational information processor and therefore a typical cybernetic system. We can look at the human being and try to extract what is likely to prove most useful.

First of all we think of input, and all the ways in which information can be sensed. We can use human eyes, radar scanners, etc. The basic problem is always that of pattern recognition. The problem is to perceive and to recognize objects, processes and indeed all sorts of events.

The main point about the input is that it is never independent of what is in the central processor or human brain. The brain's job is to compare the snapshots (in the case of vision) with its stored record of previous snapshots, perhaps so that literally it can say 'snap' when an identification occurs; perhaps more often to recognize that the event comes within a general class of events and sometimes to say that it does not have a class ready to receive this new item—it must therefore produce one.

Central processing receives much more by way of symbolized information than by snapshots. We, as human beings, learn more facts from other people's descriptions than we do by directly perceiving things. In any case, we can set a symbolized representation of a picture by describing it.

Given that we have many symbolic models in store, which are mostly in language although many can be in mathematical form, then it is natural for us to draw inferences from those symbolic models. This is why mathematical methods for assessing probabilities and risks, and making inferences are an essential part of any information processing. This goes hand in hand with the ability to converse with other people or other computers.

It can be seen from this that human-like thinking is the target, and we believe that this is largely brought about by building upon the adaptive feature of learning. The main superstructure is that of symbolization.

It is these features, some parts of which we have discussed in this book, which can be brought together to make up a model of *artificial intelligence*. In the end artificial intelligence is the central problem of cybernetics. The aspect of cybernetics we have not discussed lies in bringing together various features such as learning, information theory, perception, etc., all of which we have discussed so far in relative isolation.

Cybernetics deals with a whole set of methods in isolation which can be of enormous use to individuals who use them to help in the solution of a whole variety of problems which occur in virtually every walk of life.

Cybernetics also promotes a way of thinking. It insists on thinking in dynamic terms and dwells on the adaptive and evolutionary types of system. Plans and decisions of the most complicated kind, as in the case of our military commander in Chapter 10, are often contingent and dynamic, and must deal with changing circumstances.

The next stage of cybernetics lies in bringing all these features together to make a complete set of artificially intelligent systems.

We should say that the individual models and methods already used will be improved and new methods developed. But at the same time they will be brought together for the purpose of constructing larger and larger autonomous systems.

Another view is to say that in the future we shall be passing more and more into man-machine co-operation, and gradually this will be superseded by a 'machine only' controlling system.

The impact of cybernetics on society is another issue

which we have not, in this book, had the space to explore. It must be a speculative matter, and also a very complex matter, but it does at least seem certain that in the future man's role is likely to change very markedly, and perhaps in a very dramatic manner.

We must expect far more work in the short-term, especially of a scientific character, and far more leisure in the long term. The long term leisure is a reminder that, whereas cybernetics will allow us to escape from tedious and routine activities, it confronts us with the possibility of extreme boredom.

Applied cybernetics we think of as automation, even though historically the development of automatic control systems has preceded the cybernetic ideas which were implicit in their construction. At this stage in development, more and more do we find the cybernetic ideas taking precedence over the automatic control systems. This itself is likely to increase dramatically the rate of development of automation, or what is better called cybernation.

We may expect that all the subjects mentioned in this book, as well as a few more besides, will develop very rapidly in the future. We shall also expect to find more and more complicated models being constructed— mostly by bigger and better computers—which show all the features of perception, learning, thinking, etc., operating together. The total effect of this will be to change the face of the society in which we live.

One requirement for achieving this is that we should be educating more cyberneticians. At the moment there are very few departments of cybernetics in existence at the universities of the world. This is something which must change in the next decade. This change will come as people recognise more and more that cybernetics is, perhaps, the major science and that it should take priority over other sciences such as physics and chemistry.

We may assume that cybernetics will provide us with a scientific strength that will transform our technological know-how during the next twenty years. As a result of cybernetics, nothing will ever be quite the same again. All the changes involved will not make life easier automatically, although many will; in any case all are inevitable. We can not turn our backs on evolution.

Of all the features of cybernetic development the social impact must be the greatest. This is something we have *not* been able to deal with in this book and have merely hinted at from time to time. But it may be assumed that we shall achieve, as a result of cybernetics, a very much more complex society in the future; we will certainly, as a result, have an enormous number of problems to solve. There can be no turning back and the only way in which we can be successful is for more and more people to have a more and more complete understanding of what is virtually a science of sciences: cybernetics.

APPENDIX

FURTHER READING

AMOSOV, N. M., Modelling and Thinking and the Mind, Spartan Books, 1967.

APTER, M. J., Cybernetics and Development, Pergamon Press, 1966.

ARBIB, M. A., Brains, Machines and Mathematics, McGraw Hill, 1964.

ASHBY, W. R., Design for a Brain, Chapman and Hall, 1954.

— An Introduction to Cybernetics, Chapman and Hall, 1956.

BEER, S., Cybernetics and Management, English Universities Press, 1959.

— Decision and Control, Wiley, 1966.

BOOTH, A. D., Digital Computers in Action, Pergamon Press, 1965.

DE LATIL, P., Thinking by Machine, Sidgwick and Jackson, 1956.

FIEGENBAUM, E. A. and FELDMAN, J., Computers and Thought, McGraw Hill, 1963.

GEORGE, F. H., The Brain as a Computer, Pergamon Press, 1961.

— Cybernetics and Biology, Oliver and Boyd, 1965.

— Models of Thinking, George Allen & Unwin, 1969.

— Science and the Crisis in Society, Wiley, 1970.

HUNT, E. B., Concept Learning: An Information Processing Problem, Wiley, 1962.

KLIR, J. and VALACH, M., Cybernetic Modelling, Iliffe, 1967.

LERNER, Y., Fundamentals of Cybernetics, Science Press, 1970.

MINSKY, M., Computation: Finite and Infinite Machines, Prentice Hall, 1967.

PASK, A. G. S., An Approach to Cybernetics, Hutchinson, 1961.

PORTER, A., Cybernetics Simplified, Unibooks, 1969.

SASS, M. A. and WILKINSON, W. D., Computer Augmentation of Human Reasoning, Spartan Books, 1965.

TOMKINS, S. S. and MESSICK, S., Computer Simulation of Personality, Wiley, 1963.

WALTER, W. G., The Living Brain, Duckworth, 1953.

WIENER, N., Cybernetics, Wiley, 1st Ed. 1948, 2nd Ed. 1961.

INDEX